BECOMING THE SIGN

Sacramental Living in a Post-Conciliar Church

KATHLEEN HUGHES, RSCJ

**2012 Madeleva Lecture
in Spirituality**

Paulist Press
New York / Mahwah, NJ

Excerpts from the English translation of *The Sacramentary (Revised Edition)* © 1997, International Commission on English in the Liturgy Corporation (ICEL); excerpts from the English translation of *The Roman Missal* © 2010, ICEL. All rights reserved.

Cover and book design by Lynn Else

Library of Congress Cataloging-in-Publication Data

Hughes, Kathleen, 1942–
    Becoming the sign : sacramental living in a post-conciliar church / Kathleen Hughes, RSCJ.
      pages cm. — (2012 Madeleva lecture in spirituality)
      ISBN 978-0-8091-4824-0 (alk. paper) — ISBN 978-1-58768-233-9
      1. Catholic Church—Liturgy. 2. Liturgical reform. I. Title.
      BX1975.H84 2013
      264'.02—dc23

                                                                    2012042401

ISBN: 978-0-8091-4824-0 (paperback)
ISBN: 978-1-58768-233-9 (e-book)

Published by Paulist Press
997 Macarthur Boulevard
Mahwah, New Jersey 07430

www.paulistpress.com

Printed and bound in the
United States of America

the Sign BECOMING THE SIGN **Becoming the Sign** Becoming the Sign BECOMING

You bring the bread, I'll bring the wine. Together we will feed God's people.

We will place for them a picnic on the sacred ground of being...picnics are for eating anywhere, and so the holiness becomes reality, and all can share.

You bring the bread, and I'll bring the wine. Together we will feed God's people.

Patricia Hughes Baumer
1975

This work is dedicated
with love and gratitude
to my sisters:
Patricia Hughes Baumer
and
the Religious of the Sacred Heart of Jesus.
In endlessly varied ways
these women have been sacrament to me
helping me discover and celebrate
the love of God made visible
in Jesus Christ,
in events,
in personal encounters,
in the light and the shadows
of our ordinary days,
and in all of created reality.

CONTENTS

INTRODUCTION

Perhaps there was a certain inevitability in my giving a Madeleva lecture one day. I have a unique
connection to Sister Mary Madeleva Wolf, CSC,
the visionary president of Saint Mary's College
(1934–1961), who first made it possible for the
laity and women religious to study the sacred sci-
ences in the United States by founding the Graduate
School of Theology at St. Mary's in 1943. Sister
Mary Madeleva was a medievalist, an educator, a
speaker, and a writer. She was the author of numerous scholarly books and essays, and, at least once
a month for many years, she wrote and published
a poem "in some good magazine." As she said,
"My words have had to work for a living."[1] Thus
did she become widely known across the United
States as a poet of distinction.

As a grateful tribute to Sister Mary Madeleva
when she died in 1964, many religious orders of
women pledged to name one of their young religious after her and they looked in their ranks for
a budding poet. My sister Patricia had recently
joined the Ursuline Sisters of Cleveland, and by a
lovely serendipity, she was a writer and a poet.

She was given the religious name Sister Mary Madeleva, OSU.

The letter of invitation I received to give the Madeleva lecture in 2012 indicated that I was to address the sacramental life, approaching it from whatever specific perspective I preferred. Where to begin? What could I say that might make a difference? I suspect it was the wisdom of advancing years that made me decide this was the moment to try to make a contribution not to the world of scholarship but rather to the worship life of the American church, a church in crisis in the present day.

In the mid-1960s the Second Vatican Council profoundly transformed the religious landscape: the council promoted rapprochement with the modern world, identification with its joys and its sufferings, interreligious dialogue, a language of tolerance and understanding, a church opening its windows so that the Spirit could blow through. Truly the spirit of aggiornamento was in the air. And nowhere across the world were the reforms of the council received with as much delight and implemented with as much relish and competence as in the United States of America. There was new life and there was energy and there was an outpouring of hope. That energy and life, that fresh vision of ourselves as church, that great awakening to the mysteries we celebrate began nearly fifty years ago, yet it has waned in our day. What has happened to the post-conciliar vitality of the church in the United States in recent years?

Fast forward to the present and the sorry sight that greets us. The fallout from sexual abuse has been intense and has rocked the church to its foundations. This is a crisis of such monumental proportions that it will be years, decades even, before the toll in lives destroyed, ecclesial credibility gravely compromised, and a church in serious financial distress is in any way ameliorated.

Already though, before the sexual abuse revelations, disaffection with the church was growing. Over the last several decades the number of practicing Catholics in the United States has dwindled. According to the Pew Forum on Religion and Public Life, 28 percent of Americans have changed denominations from the church of their childhood; roughly 10 percent of Americans today are former Catholics.[2] I find that astonishing. We have been so intent on the growing clergy shortage that we have missed what seems to be an equally significant trend. Let's call it the "laity shortage"— people simply drifting away in search of spiritual nourishment elsewhere or people choosing to leave religious affiliation behind.

There is, indeed, the parallel clergy shortage. According to a Georgetown poll,[3] more than three out of ten Catholics say they have been personally affected by the clergy shortage. The latest statistics I have found indicate that over 18 percent of parishes are now without a resident pastor. Since 1995, more than eight hundred parishes have closed, most since 2000.

Who is asking why? Who is wondering whether both parishioners and potential priestly vocations have been driven away by the very public intramural battles of our church: the silencing of theologians; the skirmishes about which politicians should be denied communion; the fierce debates about potential graduation speakers at Catholic colleges and universities; the clash of positions in the health-care debate; the investigation of the Leadership Conference of Women Religious and the parallel apostolic visitation of American women religious to determine if communities are being faithful to the vows and vision they once embraced; the anomaly of welcoming married Episcopal priests and allowing their continued ministry while maintaining the discipline of celibacy; the question of women's role, still a controversial issue thirty-four years after the Vatican forbade discussion of women's ordination; dioceses facing bankruptcy and choosing layoffs, parish closings, and mergers, leading, in some instances, to acrimonious lawsuits. All of this has been very public and very contentious and, for many, both sad and demoralizing.

In the church, just as in our country, there is a general hardening of ideological positions and an astonishing lack of civility among us. There are

4

different camps on almost every issue of any import and there is a fair amount of distrust and fear. Some Web sites are positively venomous, using language as angry and hectoring as the rhetoric of the political extreme. The church is mirroring the culture of the country in its shift from dialogue and debate to diatribe and denunciation.

And all of our divisions are played out when we gather for worship. The liturgy is, of its very nature, a perfectly condensed statement of our identity and our beliefs as the Body of Christ. When we gather for worship we bring to public ritual expression our understanding of, and relationship with, the God of our Lord Jesus Christ, our understanding of the Body of Christ and how we relate to one another, and our understanding of the holy, of authority, of inclusion, and a host of other core beliefs. All of this is enacted in the liturgical event—in the choices we make, the arrangement of space, the ways and times we sit and stand, the ministers positioned before us, the focus of the homily, the music we select, the amount of liturgical participation we promote, the pattern of reception of communion, and even the register of the language we select.

Week after week we gather for the praise and glory of God. We gather to enact the saving mystery of Christ's death and rising in the power of their abundant and life-giving Spirit. But while *what* we celebrate is generally agreed on, *how* we celebrate it is the subject of wildly divergent and divisive views and choices. Our increasingly fractious communities are being deeply affected by the present contentious environment of the country and the church.

What could revitalize our lives as people of faith?

I have a conviction that a new and more penetrating understanding of the sacramental life of the church and the sacramental living it fosters and celebrates has the potential to ameliorate some of our present-day malaise. I am convinced that the sacramental vision of Vatican II has never been thoroughly catechized, nor have its implications for our lives as members of the one Body of Christ been embraced. I believe that the liturgical life of the church has the unique potential for the transformation of our attitudes and values, our relationships and responsibilities, if we recognize that it is—or should be—*radically continuous* with our everyday lives, hallowing and celebrating everyday experience, inviting deeper participation in the mystery of God with us, and committing us to live faithfully that which we have expressed in word and ritual action each time we gather for worship.

The brilliant liturgist Ralph A. Keifer (1940–1987)—scholar, writer, editor, ecumenist—once concluded his assessment of the liturgical reforms of Vatican II by suggesting that the most significant of the myriad changes introduced by the council was the repositioning of the altar to face the assembly. When we gather for the Eucharist, he noted, we enact a vision of church. The priest is no longer the sole mediator of grace, of our relationship with God. We gather facing each other, all of us concelebrants, all making the sign of God's presence to one another, all of us forming the Body of Christ, the catholic community, a discipleship of equals. And this gathering of equals before God at the table of the Eucharist sets up the perhaps unconscious expectation that these same relationships and roles will exist outside of Eucharist as well, with each one having a voice, a role, an opportunity for dialogue, an experience of collaboration and collegiality, each one of us a sacrament to others, each one of us a minister within and beyond the community, each one of us co-responsible for the mission of the church and for contributing to its flourishing.

I would add to Keifer's insight that each one of us has a *sacramental* ministry. We are all priests in virtue of our baptism. We share analogously in the ministry of unity that the sacrament of orders confers. Therefore we have both a vocation and an obligation to address the sad disarray of the community. We have a responsibility to foster the dignity of each member in the one body, to exercise in our everyday lives the reverence and hospitality that are marks of sacramental living. As I shall discuss in what follows, "full, conscious, and active participation" does not simply express an expectation of our *liturgical* involvement. "Full, conscious, and active participation" is a commitment we make to *personal involvement in the life of the church* and its continuous coming to be in this present age.

Because of this vision of church and of our co-responsibility for its vitality, I have chosen to examine sacrament through the following lens: "Becoming the Sign: Sacramental Living in a Post-Conciliar Church." This investigation is divided into five parts.

First, I will situate the Second Vatican Council in its context. Vatican II is surely the most significant event in the life of the church since the Reformation of the sixteenth century. It seems appropriate, in this fiftieth anniversary year of the council's opening, to reflect on what happened in 1962 when more than two thousand bishops convened from all over the globe and—as their first order of business—addressed the theme of the church's liturgical life. Three things in particular seem important to note: the context of the world in the mid-twentieth century when the council convened, the maturity of the liturgical movement on the eve of the council, and the respectful collaboration of bishops and scholars during those defining days.

Second, I will summarize the new vision of the church's sacramental life, a vision the council initiated in articulating certain fundamental principles. This new vision was the result of theological, historical, and pastoral investigations into each element of the liturgy; it was informed by the general laws governing ritual behavior; and it was also the product of liturgical experiment and communal reflection among those who were significant participants in the liturgical movement of the twentieth century.

Third, I will offer a definition of sacrament that takes these foundational principles seriously and I will demonstrate how this definition plays out, *mutatis mutandis*, in each of the sacraments.

Fourth, I will assess the reception of the liturgical reforms of the Second Vatican Council in the church of the United States. It was the desire of the council fathers to "...impart an ever increasing vigor to the Christian life of the faithful...."[4] It is important to ask the "so what" question: if the liturgical life of the church has been revitalized, and so much energy has been expended in its implementation, why are we not appreciably more just and more loving? I want to consider the strengths and weaknesses of the liturgical reform and its obvious unfinished sacramental agenda. And in the process, since I can't help myself as a member for nineteen years of the Advisory Committee of the International Commission on English in the Liturgy, I will speak briefly about the new translation guidelines and their deleterious effect on our sacramental imagination.

Fifth, I will propose questions that must be explored and issues that must be addressed if sacramental living is to prosper in our day. I will also suggest simple, concrete ways of forging the connections between sacramental liturgy and sacramental life, and I will offer a few directions forward so that we might truly "Become the Sign" for one another.

Part I

THE COUNCIL IN CONTEXT

The World of the Council

I begin with an oft-repeated story told to me by the late Father Godfrey Diekmann (1908–2002), a Benedictine monk of St. John's Abbey in Collegeville, Minnesota, a scholar and teacher of patristics, and, for nearly sixty years, a true champion of the liturgical movement in North America. Godfrey was a consultant to the Pontifical Liturgical Commission, one of the preparatory commissions of Vatican II. He was a *peritus* at the council—one of the "experts" invited to assist the bishops—during three of its four sessions, and he was a member of the consilium responsible for implementing the council's new liturgical vision by preparing each of the reformed liturgical rites. He was also my mentor and friend.

Godfrey described to me the day he sat in the balcony of St. Peter's where the votes were being taken on the Constitution on the Sacred Liturgy, chapter by chapter. He was astonished at the outcome of the council's deliberations—a reform of the church's liturgy well beyond anything that the leaders of the liturgical movement could have asked for or even imagined. There was, in this text, more solid, contemporary theology, more possibility for the vernacular, more lay participation. There was, in fact, the promise of more genuine liturgical reform and renewal than anyone had anticipated. And, as each chapter came up for a vote, it received virtually unanimous approval from the world's bishops.

That evening Godfrey joined some United States bishops for a great celebratory dinner at the Cavaleri Hilton on the outskirts of Rome. They were a jubilant group, toasting first this amendment and then that triumph. At one point a woman leaned over from a table nearby and asked them: "Aren't you all Americans? Don't you know your president was shot today?" As Godfrey recalled, they all got up from the table and went out into the night, searching for a church where they could celebrate a requiem Mass.

For me this story serves to ground the council in the midst of world events and reflects, too, what was happening in the American church. Kennedy's presidency was a definitive statement of a church come of age, no longer the immigrant ghetto church of the turn of the twentieth century, but a church that had produced a leader for the free world.[1] The story also conjures the heady days of the early 1960s. Naively we referred to that time as Camelot, but Camelot it decidedly was not. Here is one account of the bigger picture:

> The council was largely framed by the traumatic events of 1956 and 1968: the repression of popular uprisings by Russian tanks in Budapest and Prague. Implicit in this cold war tapestry were events that are now largely unknown to a youthful generation precisely because they are in the settled past: Hitler's aggression and the Holocaust; the Soviet empire whose seeds lay in the blood of Stalingrad; the Atomic Age that was born at Hiroshima; the postwar division of the world into two mutually exclusive ideologies and superpowers; and the ever-present threat of nuclear annihilation.[2]

The council did not happen in a vacuum. Vatican II was convened in the mid-twentieth century, surely the most violent of all centuries. The human community was in shambles. Two global wars and the Jewish holocaust had, together, claimed nearly sixty million lives. The cold war raged and the Soviet totalitarian empire covered nearly one third of the world's land. Decolonization signaled the end of Western hegemony and led to a destabilized and highly volatile Africa. With the invention of the atomic bomb human extinction had become a very real possibility.

On our own shores, the beginning of the space race and the establishment of the Peace Corps were overshadowed by the events of the Civil Rights movement, especially the anger and violence that greeted school desegregation, and by the growing wave of protest of the Vietnam War.

Furthermore, Vatican II opened just days before the darkest episode of this age—the Cuban missile crisis of 1962. For fifteen days that October, the world faced the prospect of total destruction. It was truly a terrifying time for those who lived through it.

Situating the council historically helps to capture the climate within which the council fathers assembled and, more important, the breadth of concerns among the participants. From all they had witnessed, the bishops must have brought with them deep apprehensions about the world's fragmentation and its seeming heartless inhumanity, realizations which surely affected some of their liturgical insights about the centrality of the death and rising of Jesus, about the importance of the Mystical Body and our responsibilities to one another in the human community, and about participation in the sacraments as a solemn commitment to a way of being in the world, laboring for the vision and the values of the reign of God.

As I consider the perilous state of the world in the early 1960s, I wonder whether it may have been these very cataclysmic events which *embold-*

ened the bishops to engage in a council unlike any other in the history of the church—in length, in numbers of participants and their global representation, in the quantity and quality of conciliar debate, in the number of documents issued and the tone of their rhetoric, and, above all, in the decision to speak not just to one another behind closed doors but to the whole of the human community, offering a word of healing and hope.[3]

Pope John XXIII had announced two aims for the council: first, to promote "the enlightenment, edification, and joy of the entire Christian people," and second, "to extend a renewed cordial invitation to the faithful of the separated churches to participate with us in this feast of grace and brotherhood." Then the windows were thrown wide open! This council was to be good news to Catholics of every state of life, to Christians of other traditions, to believers and non-believers, and to all people of good will. From the beginning, Vatican II was a council that would address both the internal and the external affairs of the church. It was a council in dialogue with the whole world.

In addressing, even embracing, the world, the council clearly needed a new mode of communication. The style of discourse characteristic of councils from Nicaea through Vatican I would never do. The choice of rhetoric adopted by Vatican II is a stunning departure from previous conciliar communication. There is little trace of warning or condemnation, nor is there an adversarial stance vis-à-vis the council's conversation partners. Rather, Vatican II employs a pastoral style of invitation, persuasion, and dialogue. The bishops chose a posture of openness and conversation with the world as essential to the very mission of the church. The language of the conciliar documents is, on the whole, warm and familial.[4]

I think of this new literary style as a form of homiletic for, like a good homily, the style of discourse adopted by Vatican II is heart speaking to heart—*cor ad cor loquitur*. The tone is one of mutuality: we are in this together, all of us called to holiness after the manner of Jesus Christ, and all of us called to engagement with the world for its continual flourishing. The council fathers held up an image of who we are called to be with the hope that hearts would be touched and moved to action. The rhetoric of Vatican II is both an invitational and an adult model of exhortation.

This may sound like a completely idealized vision of the council's discourse. True, the documents are not uniformly invitational. Besides, they reflect inconsistencies, even contradictions. They are certainly not all in the style of homiletic. The bishops began numerous conversations but left a fair number of open questions or partial answers. The documents are also uneven in the enduring value of their content. Consider, for example, the Decree on the Instruments of Social Communications, which, given the technological revolution, can seem quaint and from another age altogether. But by and large we can find in the sixteen documents of the council "enlightenment, edification and joy" as Pope John XXIII had hoped, and we are offered a truly amazing banquet of reflections on matters large and small, a genuine "feast of grace."

The Maturity of the Liturgical Movement

A second important context for the council's reform of the liturgy was the convergence of new scholarship in a variety of fields. The twentieth century witnessed a biblical revitalization, the renewal of patristic studies, the development of the social gospel in light of Leo XIII's writings, the stirrings of an ecumenical movement, and, in particular for our purposes, the maturity of the liturgical movement, dependent in many ways on the insights of all of these other fields.

There were different phases to the liturgical movement. Virgil Funk describes this movement as "a century-long effort made to enrich the appreciation and experience of worship," and he makes a helpful distinction between a movement and a formal organization. Movements "...follow a cycle beginning with issues, widening into a cause, coming to a climax or confrontation, and being absorbed into a new or existing organization."[5]

That cycle was clearly played out in the decades leading up to and including the council.

There were a variety of key players in the liturgical movement including monks, scholars, pastors, practitioners, legislators, and activists, each in turn adding to the rich dialogue in key ways. From a quiet beginning in several Benedictine communities in Europe interested in the revival of Gregorian chant and the more faithful unfolding of the key events of the liturgical year, the movement gradually developed its core emphasis, namely, the restoration of the laity's active participation in the liturgical life of the church.

There were newly discovered ancient treatises that included fascinating descriptions of developing liturgical practice among the early Christian communities. Scholars were able to determine the earliest patterns of the eucharistic prayer, the various phases of the initiation of adult converts, the gradual evolution and rich variety of patterns of the church's penitential practices over the centuries, the ritual roots of marriage in domestic practices long before marriage was declared a sacrament, the community's pastoral care of its suffering members, and the role of the whole community in identifying and blessing members of the community for leadership. These patterns were further amplified by fresh and intriguing archeological discoveries, for example, of house churches and atriums and baptismal pools. Scholars had precious evidence of the Christian community's evolving ritual patterns, the language of its prayer, the ministries involved, the spaces used. All of this was critical material for the thorough historical, theological, and pastoral investigation of the church's patterns of prayer that was necessary before the reform of the rites was possible.

At the same time there were theologians and biblical scholars whose writings probed for deeper understanding of Christ as the primordial sacrament, the Spirit as mediating graced relationship, and the world as gift and task. Most seminal, of course, were the writings of Edward Schillebeeckx, particularly his major work *Christ the Sacrament of the Encounter with God*. Schillebeeckx's lens was that of Christology. His focus was on the relationship between Christ and the church, and on sacraments as moments of encounter with Christ rather than objects dispensing grace. His work profoundly influenced the Constitution on the Sacred Liturgy and subsequent sacramental and liturgical theology.

The twentieth century also witnessed significant papal interventions that advanced the liturgical movement, especially from Pius X and Pius XII. In 1903, Pius X published a *motu proprio* that stated:

> As it is indeed our most fervent wish that the true Christian spirit should flourish again in every field and be upheld by all the faithful, we should

above all be mindful of the sanctity and dignity of the Church building; for it is there that the faithful meet to draw that same spirit from its most important and indispensable source, *active participation in the sacred mysteries and in the public and solemn prayer of the Church.*[6]

In the next several years Pius X underscored one of the most important aspects of active participation by encouraging more frequent reception of communion and by lowering the age for the reception of first Eucharist to the "age of reason," about seven.

Two encyclicals of Pius XII also provided theological foundations for and a mainstream credibility to the liturgical movement. *Mystici Corporis* (1943) promoted an ecclesiology of the church as the Mystical Body of Christ, an ecclesiology given voice in the council's Dogmatic Constitution on the Church and underpinning the community's social responsibility enacted in the Eucharist. United with Christ and with one another, members of the Body of Christ are taken up into communion with Christ and with one another in the sharing of the Eucharist, and this binds us in solidarity in daily life and pledges our responsibility one to another.[7]

Four years later Pius XII promulgated *Mediator Dei* (1947), the first encyclical in the history of the church whose central theme was the liturgy. While pointing out certain errors and excesses, Pius XII firmly allied himself with the liturgical movement, and his encyclical gave support and energy to those calling for liturgical reform.

Perhaps most significant of all these restless stirrings of the twentieth century were the liturgical conferences and study weeks that were convened, first in Europe and then in North America. We cannot underestimate the importance of these gatherings where scholarly research was placed in dialogue with the experience of believers and the needs of the world. "The Family in Christ," "Christ's Sacrifice and Ours," "The Sanctification of Sunday," "The Bible and the Liturgy," "The Liturgy and Unity in Christ" were some of the theological themes addressed. Workshops that followed presentations on these topics, particularly in the United States, took a decidedly practical and pastoral turn. During these conferences, especially the international study weeks, dialogue was vigorous and consensus was building among liturgical leaders about the key goals of a liturgical reform.

In 1956 the Assisi Study Week and the Congress that followed drew more than fourteen hundred participants from five continents, including more than eighty bishops and six cardinals. It has been suggested that the Assisi Congress was "...pivotal for what would transpire liturgically at the Second Vatican Council because when the time came to formulate the invitation list for the preparatory commission on the liturgy, it was precisely the Assisi roster of participants that was consulted."[8]

The men who formed the preparatory commission on the liturgy knew and respected one another as colleagues and, often, as friends. They had thoroughly debated the shape of the various rites. They were in nearly complete accord that active participation must be restored to the assembly, that the rites must be simple and transparent, that the priesthood of all believers must be promoted, and that the education of clergy and laity alike was essential to the full flowering of a renewed liturgy. Their work on thirteen subcommissions led to a schema that was the first document presented to the council fathers for discussion and adoption.

The Collaboration of Bishops and Theologians in the Work of the Council

Besides the context of the world in the mid-twentieth century and the maturity of the liturgical movement on the eve of the council, there is a third remarkable circumstance of Vatican II that deserves to be noted. In the midst of the hundreds who gathered for the council were a number of theologians welcomed into the council's deliberations who, on its eve, had been banned from speaking, theologians whose views had previously been condemned. Among these influential theologians, once silenced, were Karl Rahner, Henri de Lubac, Yves Congar, and John Courtney Murray.

Bishop Denis Hurley of Durban, South Africa, once referred to the contributions of these giants, along with those of countless other theologians invited by individual bishops, as "...one of the greatest adult education programs ever run!" During the day, the bishops exercised their teaching office. Then, night after night, roles were reversed. All over Rome there were countless gatherings large and small where theologians were sought out by the bishops to help them prepare for the next day's work. The Second Vatican Council provided a compelling image of bishops and theologians learning from one another—everyone a teacher, everyone a learner—both as eager to listen as to teach, both knowing limitations and need of the other in a spirit of reciprocity and humility. New theological insights found willing minds and hearts.

The time was ripe for change. After sometimes fierce debate[9] in fifteen general congregations with 297 written proposals and 328 oral interventions, the Constitution on the Sacred Liturgy received an astonishing affirmation by the assembled bishops: 2,147 in favor; four opposed.[10] On December 4, 1963, the Constitution on the Sacred Liturgy became the first document promulgated by the Second Vatican Council.

In light of the virtually unanimous support for the Constitution on the Sacred Liturgy in 1963, those naysayers today who are trying to promote a "reform of the reform" of worship need to explain how they think the council was hijacked by a rump group of wild-eyed radicals. It appears far more likely that the council was hijacked by the Holy Spirit.

Part II

PRINCIPLES OF THE LITURGICAL REFORM

Before turning to the church's sacramental life, I want to propose a framework of significant principles that undergirds our sacramental renewal.[1] By far the most important principle, and the heart of the liturgical reform, is captured in article 5 of the Constitution on the Sacred Liturgy:

> God who "wills that all be saved and come to the knowledge of the truth" (1 Tm 2:4), "who in many and various ways spoke in times past to the fathers by the prophets" (Heb 1:1), when the fullness of time had come sent His Son, the Word made flesh, anointed by the Holy Spirit, to preach the Gospel to the poor, to heal the contrite of heart; he is "the physician, being both flesh and of the Spirit," the mediator between God and us. For his humanity, united with the person of the Word, was the instrument of our salvation. Therefore in Christ "the perfect achievement of our reconciliation" came forth and the fullness of divine worship was given to us."

The wonderful works of God among the people of the Old Testament were a prelude to the work of Christ the Lord. He achieved His task of redeeming humanity and giving perfect glory to God principally by the paschal mystery of his blessed passion, resurrection from the dead, and glorious ascension, whereby "dying, he destroyed our death and, rising, he restored our life." For it was from the side of Christ as he slept the sleep of death upon the cross that there came forth the sublime sacrament of the whole Church.[2]

These paragraphs ground the renewal of the church's liturgical life in Christ's incarnation as well as in his redemptive act, and in what is called "the sublime sacrament of the whole Church." Christ and church, two sacraments from which flow seven privileged means of encounter with the divine.

I think again of my friend Godfrey Diekmann. Long before Edward Schillebeeckx wrote of Christ as the sacrament of our encounter with God, Godfrey was passionately promoting the same idea. One night in the mid-1990s we were discussing theology over dinner when Godfrey slammed the table for effect and shouted, "It's the incarnation, dammit!" As you can imagine, people at neighboring tables were a bit startled. Godfrey was right. All sacramental living is possible because God became human in Jesus of Nazareth, who by his life, death, and rising hallowed all of human life. Or, as Pierre Teilhard de Chardin describes it in his lyrical *Hymn of the Universe*, the incarnation effected the transubstantiation of the whole world. Jesus is the perfect revelation of the heart of God, the enabler of our encounter with the Father in the power of the Spirit. Jesus Christ is the perfect sacrament. And the church is the sacramental embodiment of Christ's continued presence and activity in the world. The sacraments of the church are particular, condensed celebrations of the human encounter with the divine. Sacraments both discover and manifest the experience of the holy in daily life, and they help to strengthen the connection between liturgy and life. Each sacrament is radically continuous with the experience of human life transformed by Christ.

There are other important principles the council addressed as foundational for the reform of the sacramental rites. Let me highlight them briefly:

1. *The heart of every liturgical celebration is the celebration of the paschal mystery of Christ for the life of the world and our participation in one or another facet of that event.*

As the Constitution on the Sacred Liturgy reminds us: "...the effect of the sacraments and sacramentals is that almost every event in [our] lives is made holy by divine grace that flows from the paschal mystery of Christ's passion, death, and resurrection, the fount from which all sacraments and sacramentals draw their

27

power." And further, "...there is hardly any proper use of material things that cannot thus be directed toward human sanctification and the praise of God."[3]

The constitution thus underscores that every time the church gathers for the liturgy, it is first and foremost a celebration of the life, death, and rising of Jesus Christ, whose incarnation illuminates and transforms all created reality, and whose dying and rising gives meaning to the daily dying and rising, the pain and joy, the suffering and hope that is part of every person's daily existence. Material things, events, and encounters are all the stuff of holiness and all of them have the possibility of giving glory to God. *Every liturgy is an exercise of the priestly office of Jesus Christ, head and members, for the glory of God and the sanctification of humankind.* This principle the constitution develops emphatically when it proclaims that "...the liturgy is considered as an exercise of the priestly office of Jesus Christ. In the liturgy, by means of signs perceptible to the senses, human sanctification is signified and brought about in ways proper to each of these signs; in the liturgy the whole public worship is performed by the Mystical Body of Jesus Christ, that is, by the Head and his members."[4]

2. From this, it follows that *all members of the assembly, priestly people through baptism, and members of the Mystical Body of Jesus, are co-presiders with Christ, the one and only high priest and leader of prayer.*

It is Jesus Christ, the high priest, who stands before the throne of grace interceding on our behalf. It is Jesus Christ who joins us to himself in one body, gathered to give praise and glory to God. This principle does not suggest that there are not particular offices and ministries within the assembly. It simply underscores that the members of the assembly are not passive spectators as the priest-presider celebrates the ritual. On the contrary, the celebrant "…associates the people with himself in the offering of sacrifice through Christ in the Holy Spirit to God the Father."[5] We had been schooled, prior to Vatican II, to think of the priest as the mediator between God and the human community; now, however, no longer are members of the assembly gathered there as "strangers or silent spectators."[6] The *General Instruction on the Roman Missal* underscores the meaning of the phrase "priestly people" and clarifies our role thus: "…the faithful form a holy people, a people of God's own possession and a royal Priesthood, so that they may give thanks to God and offer the unblemished sacrificial Victim not only by means of the hands of the Priest but also together with him and so that they may learn to offer their very selves."[7] The corollary of being a priestly people in the liturgy, of course, is that members of the community are priests as well in daily life, a point to which we will return.

3. *In the liturgy Christ is present in many ways— in the bread and wine, in the word proclaimed, in the ministers, and, not least, in the assembly gathered for prayer and praise. In other words, we make Christ present to each other when we come together.*[8]

By this principle, the council fathers broke open the meaning of sacrament. To Christ's presence under the appearance of bread and wine—the traditional localization of the "real presence" —the constitution adds Christ's presence in the other sacraments, in the proclamation of the word of God, in the ministers of the liturgy, and in the assembly of faithful people gathered for prayer. The meaning of "presence" is enlarged to include the presence of Christ in material signs, in the word spoken and embraced, and in those standing around us at the altar. Again, there is a corollary in the way God's presence is made manifest in daily life through words, objects, and our human presence to one another. It is truly an awesome thought that we, too, are the "real presence" to one another.

The liturgy is the most perfect manifestation of the church. The mystery of Christ is made visible when God's holy people actively participate in the same Eucharist, at a single altar, each according to his or her role. "Church" is not an abstraction but a tangible reality when a community at worship is a sign of Christ's presence with one another. For that very reason, communal celebrations of the rites are always to be preferred to private or quasi-private events.[9] In the reform of the individual sacraments, communal forms of the rite are included as options and, in most instances, are the preferred form.

Each sacrament has an ecclesial and a mission dimension. In other words, each sacrament builds up the body of believers and is a witness to its members and, at the same time, each sacrament is a commitment to a way of being in the world. This principle articulating the internal and external aspects of the sacraments has been spelled out carefully in the Dogmatic Constitution on the Church, another rich though less well-known locus for sacramental reflection.[10] There is always a double movement in the sacraments. Engagement in the sacraments transforms individuals and the community as a whole. Simultaneously, sacraments propel us beyond ourselves to manifest to all the saving power of God in the here and now.

The liturgy is the fount and the summit of Christian life.[11] Evangelization, conversion, and faith find their ultimate expression in the liturgy, which, in turn, is the source of all holiness. At the same time, liturgical participation commits one to a life of faithful discipleship. Liturgical spirituality is rooted in this realization of the centrality of the liturgy in the Christian life. Other spiritual exercises, such as contemplation or private devotions, will be oriented to the liturgy and derived from its true spirit.[12] All that we are, all that we believe and hope and long for, finds ultimate expression in the sacraments, and, in turn, the sacraments commit us to a way of life in which we live in the day-to-day what we have proclaimed in word and rite.

4. *Sacraments are thus both intensive and extensive over time.*

This is a wholly new way of conceiving the church's sacramental life. Pre-conciliar attention to the matter and form of the sacrament tended to attenuate the reality of sacrament; its process nature was little understood or developed. As shall be discussed below, each sacrament is a ritual celebration (the intensive aspect) of an experience that has gradually developed over time—for example, coming to faith or readiness to bind oneself to another. And in the celebration, the sacrament elicits a commitment to a new, graced relationship

31

with self, others, and, above all, God (the extensive aspect, taking place long after word and rite cease).

Further, to speak of sacraments as intensive and extensive names the process nature of the sacramental experience. Sacraments do not happen in a vacuum. Sacraments presume and are built on ordinary life experience that they ritualize, strengthen, and extend. We shall explore the process nature of the sacraments below.

5. *The "grace" of the sacrament is God's self-communication in love.*

What else is grace but relationship? For too long grace was thought of as a "thing" that was quantifiable. The old catechism definition of a sacrament suggested as much: "A sacrament is an outward sign, instituted by Christ, to give grace." And grace itself, in the categories of scholastic theology, came in a variety of flavors: actual, sanctifying, prevenient, consequent, sacramental, and so on...all ways in which God meted out God's blessings. Yet, God's best blessing is not quantifiable; it is a share in God's very life. Grace is a way of union. It is an invitation to a new and deeper way of living in this sacramental universe where God longs to be in relationship with us and draws us again and again into God's very heart. Sacraments mediate encounter with the divine.

6. *To our outward ritual participation must be joined the habit of interior presence and assent.*

In light of the principle that grace is a matter of relationship, the active assent of both parties is vital. Probably no liturgical principle of the Constitution on the Sacred Liturgy has been quoted more often than the principle of full, conscious, and active participation. Long before this was articulated at Vatican II, it had been urged by Pius X at the beginning of the twentieth century and had become the battle cry of the liturgical movement.

Active participation in the liturgy is essential so that this primary and indispensable source of all holiness may achieve its end. Active participation, the right and duty of all the assembly by reason of baptism, is both internal and external. It includes verbal participation, actions, gestures, bodily attitudes, and silence. While active participation is expressed outwardly, it is *primarily* a habit of interior presence and assent,[13] enabling the liturgy to invite us into union with Christ and participation in the very life of God.

While other facets of the reform could be highlighted and further principles could be articulated, I believe that these are the foundational principles upon which the liturgical renewal was built. From our vantage point, and because particular reforms are now so familiar, it is possible to overlook how extraordinary were the principles and the mandates contained in the Constitution on the Sacred Liturgy which, in turn, produced: a new lectionary with two- and three-year cycles of readings for weekdays and Sundays respectively; the restoration of the adult catechumenate and the integrity of the sacraments of initiation; a separate rite of infant baptism drawn up to reflect the faith and commitment of the parents and the believing community; recovery of pastoral care of the sick alongside the church's ministry to the dying; revision of the rites of Christian burial; development of three rites of reconciliation reflecting pastoral practice from different ages of the church's life; recovery of the centrality of Sunday and the major feasts and seasons of the church year with a vastly simplified liturgical calendar; some simplification of the liturgy of the hours with emphasis on the sanctification of the day. And, in the celebration of the Eucharist, the renewed celebration included: the recovery of the two-part structure of the liturgy of the word and the liturgy of the Eucharist in place of emphasis on offertory, consecration, and communion, with the word as a kind of appendage; the restoration of the homily in place of a sermon on a topic of the presider's choice; the prayers of the faithful; communion under two species; and the expansion of liturgical ministries to include lay women and men principally as altar servers, readers, cantors, and ministers of communion.

Part III

SACRAMENT REIMAGINED

Before talking further about sacrament, let's pause for a moment. How do *you* define the word "sacrament"? It might be a helpful exercise to write your own definition of sacrament before going any further. Like so many other words we use so easily, it is possible to presume we mean the same thing by the term while we have widely divergent understandings. Our family upbringing, our religious instruction, our reading and reflection, and, above all, our experiences of the sacraments over a lifetime have shaped our understanding of the sacramental life of the church. I daresay the way the sacraments are celebrated, whether carefully and beautifully or in a perfunctory and minimalist manner, also contributes to our always developing understanding of the church's sacramental economy.

The Constitution on the Sacred Liturgy did not give us a definition of sacrament, strictly speaking. Yet, in light of the principles outlined in the previous section, a new way of conceiving of sacrament emerges in the constitution's vision, one that is a bit more ample and satisfying than the old *Baltimore Catechism*'s cryptic definition: "A sacrament is an outward sign, instituted by Christ to give grace,"[1] or the longer but somewhat juridical and stilted language of the *Catechism of the Catholic Church*:

> The sacraments are efficacious signs of grace, instituted by Christ and entrusted to the Church, by which divine life is dispensed to us. The visible rites by which the sacraments are celebrated signify and make present the graces proper to each sacrament. They bear fruit in those who receive them with the required dispositions.[2]

The following is the way I have come to conceive of sacrament, a definition developed over time and always open to new perceptions:

A sacrament is an event, at decisive moments in the life of the community, and through its ordered ministry, that celebrates, in symbolic language, the experience of encounter with God, in Christ, incarnate, dead and risen, through the power of the Spirit, in the life of the community and each of its members.

The celebration of sacrament brings to expression and deepens faith-filled human response to God's initiative and commits us to live what, through the ritual event, has been proclaimed until

*God has become all in all and there is no more
need of sacrament.*

Allow me to look more closely at this definition
with some elaboration:

A sacrament is an event. That means that a sacrament is a vital action; it is not a thing. It is a ritual
engagement that takes place *at decisive moments in
the life of the community.* With the exception of the
Eucharist, every sacrament marks a threshold or a
crossroads moment of human experience—for
example, the experience of embracing the faith, of
repentance and reconciliation, of serious illness and
the need for healing, of self-donation in love to
another, of vocation, and so on. These crossroads
moments are witnessed by the community and *its
ordered ministry.* Indeed, as will be discussed more
fully when we consider individual sacraments,
members of the community have a role in nurturing
the sacramental experience of one another in daily
life, a role that is genuinely part of the ordered ministry of the church.

A sacrament is a *celebration.* The word "celebration" is rooted in the Latin word *celebrare,*
which does *not* include balloons and hoopla, an
early misunderstanding that led to resistance in
speaking of "the celebration of a funeral" or "the
celebration of anointing." *Celebrare* is a word that
refers to repeated actions or ritual patterns. To celebrate means to bring a human religious experience to public, ritual expression, through the use

of *symbolic language*, including words, gestures, objects, music, and even the language of silence.

To celebrate a sacrament is an *experience of encounter with God, in Christ, incarnate, dead and risen, through the power of the Spirit, in the life of the community and its members.* Sacraments forge relationship with the triune God, each person of the Trinity active in the sacramental event, each sacrament a deepening of encounter with the divine for each individual in the assembly and for the community as the one body giving praise and glory to God.

The celebration of sacrament brings to expression; in other words, sacraments give public voice to one's experience. At the same time a sacrament cannot create experience if it does not already exist. For example, if a person goes through the motions of going to confession but has no sense of sorrow and repentance, the formula of absolution cannot create the experience of repentance or the grace and comfort of reconciliation with God and the community. We used to use the phrase "a bad confession" to describe such an event. Similarly, if a couple has not given themselves to each other in love going up the aisle, if they have not freely given and received from each other the irrevocable consent we know as the marriage covenant,[3] they have not celebrated a sacramental marriage going down the aisle. Annulments do not declare a marriage over; they declare that there never was a sacramental marriage.

Not only do sacraments bring experience to expression but they *also deepen faith-filled human experience*. The celebration of the rite deepens the human experience that it is bringing to expression. For example, in the celebration of Christian initiation—the water and word, the candle and clothing, the oil and the laying on of hands, the welcome for the first time to the table—each individual element, and all of them combined, deepen the experience of dying and rising with Christ in a community of shared faith and mission. The sense of "coming to faith" has been heightened and deepened by the ritual words and actions.

Our faith-filled human response in sacrament is *response to God's initiative*. Sacrament is, from beginning to end, God's action, God's initiative, God's invitation to a new and deeper relationship. Every sacrament, in one way or another, is an experience of conversion through which God invites us and draws us more deeply into the divine life, in faith, in trust, in service, in acceptance, in healing, in sorrow, and in all the daily ways we die and rise in union with the dying and rising of Jesus.

Every sacrament is an *act of commitment*. That's the power of the word *Amen*. We say "Amen," a word of promise and intention that binds us to live what, through the rite, has been proclaimed in word and action. "Amen." Yes, I will try to live with integrity what we have just enacted. Yes, I will strive to live faithfully in the day-to-day the promises I just recited, the trust I begged for, the love I pledged, the purpose of amendment I have experienced and expressed. And I will do this *until God has become all in all and there is no more need of sacrament*, no need, because ritual mediation of encounter is no longer necessary. I will see God face to face.

Sacraments too often are understood as that which happens at the baptism, or the anointing, or the ordination, or the wedding...the hour or so of the rite. But the sacramental rite is simply the public, ecclesial acknowledgement and celebration of what has *already* been going on in the life of the individual or group; the ritual deepens the experience and enables the individual or group to live the experience more fully and faithfully into the future *following* the public celebration. There is a ritual celebration of a sacrament that happens in the midst of the process of sacramental living; the sacramental rite is radically continuous with the sacramentality of the day-to-day. To think otherwise is to make of sacrament a kind of magic moment.

The process of each of the sacraments is more or less the same. God invites us to a new conversion of life; we experience the invitation; we are free to respond one way or the other. If we accept God's call to conversion, that invitation deepens in our lives until the point when we are prepared for the ritual celebration of what is happening. And, long after the celebration, the process continues to be played out. Each sacrament is a public ritual celebration of an experience of personal internal conversion, whether the conversion experience is one of sorrow for sin and restoration of relationship, or the need for healing of body and spirit, or the deepening of one's trust in God in the face of serious illness, or the coming to cherish another and the self-donation this demands, or the commitment to give one's life to the service of the community, and so on.

The *Rite of Christian Initiation of Adults* (RCIA) provides a model to illustrate these principles and this definition as well as to examine and interpret every other sacrament. For one thing, this rite is clearly extensive over time. The process of coming to faith takes months and sometimes even years. The RCIA is actually a whole complex of rites celebrating various thresholds in the experience of conversion and faith of the one being welcomed into the community.

In a way one could think of initiation (or any of the sacraments) as an accordion, an event stretched out over a period of time without fixed duration, an event that, step by step, takes place in the midst of the community. Gone are the private instruction classes in the pastor's study. In their place, "...the instruction catechumens receive, while presenting

41

Catholic teaching in its entirety, also enlightens faith, directs the heart toward God, fosters participation in the liturgy, inspires apostolic activity, and nurtures a life completely in accord with the spirit of Christ."[4] The emphasis of the sacrament shifts from the washing away of original sin to incorporation into the life of God, entrance into the community of faith, and commitment to a way of sacramental living.

The process of initiation takes human experience seriously. Coming to faith requires time; it is nurtured by the ministry of many others; it is celebrated in a variety of rituals (acceptance into the order of catechumens, the signing of the senses, the rite of election, prayers, exorcisms, blessings, the water bath and anointing, and finally being welcomed to the table and receiving first Eucharist) that mark various movements in this larger journey of conversion. And each of the rituals invites deeper conversion and commitment to a way of life that has only just begun.

What is so obviously a process in the initiation journey is true of other sacraments as well. Consider the experience and the process involved in the sacrament of orders. Where is a priestly vocation born? When does the process begin? The moment may be as difficult to pinpoint as the moment of falling in love for a couple. The call to serve God may be inspired by meeting a priest who is whole and holy and given to service. The call may be born in the desire to care for those who are on the margins of society. A priestly vocation may be identified in a love for the liturgy of the church or a gift for preaching. The call may be instilled by the nudge of someone asking, "Have you ever considered the priesthood?"

However the journey begins, it is even more extensive than the sacrament of initiation. There are years of study and a rigorous process of formation that involves the deepening of a life of prayer, selfless service, and growth in holiness. Along the way there are many who help to nurture the candidate's vocation, including parents and friends, teachers, counselors, and spiritual directors—all of them exercising a form of sacramental ministry with the candidate. There are examinations and testing of vocation by wise others. There are formal stages in the process, each one marked by a minor rite. Then there is the full, public, ecclesial moment of the laying on of hands and the prayer of consecration. And in the midst of the ordination, the priest makes the commitment of a lifetime: "...to unite himself more closely every day to Christ the High Priest, who offered himself for us to the Father as a perfect sacrifice."[5] The sacrament of priestly ministry continues to unfold throughout the life of the priest.

The sacrament of marriage evolves in much the same way. Love is discovered, grows, and deepens between two people who gradually discern that they have been called to share their lives with each other in undivided affection. The growing sacramental reality is marked by many ritual moments, such as celebrations of the anniversary when the couple first met and the meeting of each other's families for the first time. There is the more formal proposal, the ring, the period of engagement, the pre-Cana instruction and dialogue, the planning of the wedding ceremony, as well as all the discoveries in the endless conversations and self-disclosures that in large ways and small indicate what conversion in each one is needed to become of one heart with the other. And once a couple has publicly pledged their love for each other in the rite of marriage, they "grow into" the sacrament, bearing witness to others by the faithfulness of their love in good times and bad, in sickness and in health, all the days of their lives.

The sacraments of ordination and matrimony set those who partake of them on a lifelong journey. However long the preparation, those who approach either of these sacraments are mercifully naive about the challenges, the joys and sufferings, the disappointments along the way. The call to conversion is not once only but daily; the sacrament evolves over time while individuals choose again and again to live what they have proclaimed in word and ritual action and for which they have received the grace of the sacrament like a time-release capsule, available over a lifetime of choices.

The language of conversion is perhaps more obvious in the process of reconciliation and the sacrament of penance. We all know what St. Paul was talking about when he declared: "What I do, I do not understand. For I do not do what I want, but I do what I hate" (Rom 7:15, NABRE). In other words, that which I should do, I don't do. And that which I should not do, I specialize in! Paul knew the human condition and described it so well. Such is the struggle with which we are all too familiar.

The story of the prodigal son in the fifteenth chapter of Luke is a perfect illustration of the process of reconciliation. Whether because of curiosity or ambition or greed or simply restlessness, the son demanded his inheritance and left home. But then he got on the wrong bus and, eventually impoverished, stripped of dignity, and quite alone, he ended up feeding swine and eating from their trough. His downfall was not a single decision but a whole series of choices over a span of time. Sin is as much a process as is reconciliation.

Then the story takes a turn. The son "came to his senses" and began the journey home. What caused this conversion, this turning back? Probably the prodigal went through many stages: feeling sorry for himself, anger at his own stupidity, embarrassment that he had lost his inheritance, longing for the comforts of the home he had abandoned, and perhaps eventually sorrow that he had broken his father's heart. Something made him come to his senses. Something intrudes in our lives too, whether a sense of alienation, or the goodness of another, or the pinpricks of conscience, or sorrow, or maybe just a sense of drifting into unhealthy attitudes and practices. The process of reconciliation begins. We, like the prodigal, come to our senses and begin the journey home, longing for forgiveness and healing.

How will that be ritualized? Perhaps a heart-to-heart talk with the person we have hurt. Perhaps a conversation with a soul friend. Perhaps prayer and penance. Perhaps partaking of the Eucharist. Perhaps participation in the sacrament of reconciliation, in either a communal or private setting. The beauty of the sacrament of reconciliation is the ritual experience, both the declaration of my infidelity and desire to live a more faithful life, and the proclamation of God's mercy and forgiveness mediated by the community of believers. Then, after the ritual celebration, the experience continues: the doing of penance, the righting of wrongs, the firm purpose of amendment, the desire to live differently...there is no end to the process of sinfulness and forgiveness in all of our lives.

Happily, the sacrament of the anointing of the sick is no longer reserved to one's deathbed but is now available to anyone who is seriously ill, who faces surgery, or who experiences the debility of old age. It is a repeatable sacrament, one which, in the course of an illness, may periodically bring comfort and the assurance of the community's love and prayers. The sacrament of anointing—the prayer of faith, the laying on of hands, and the anointing with oil—is clearly part of a larger process of care and concern for the one who is ill, provided by everyone from medical personnel to family, friends, parish visitors, all of them in a variety of ways exercising a sacramental ministry, becoming the sign of God's presence and tender caress. "Every scientific effort to prolong life and every act of care for the sick, on the part of any person may be considered...a sharing in Christ's healing ministry."[6]

One of the anointing prayers describes the effects of the sacrament : courage, comfort, patience, hope, assurance of support.[7] That is the fervent prayer of the community for their loved ones, stricken by illness of any kind. Moreover, the process nature of the rite implies that all of us share in this ministry of mutual charity within the body of Christ by doing all we can to help the sick return to health and by surrounding them with love.

In summary, most of the sacraments celebrate crossroads moments of the human journey. They bring to ecclesial expression the faith community's presence and blessing at times of birth and coming of age, of vocation, of rupture and reconciliation, of sickness, old age, and death. These are the critical passages of human life, each of them a new invitation to join ourselves to Christ, a new call to conversion as turning to God or moving more deeply into the life of God.

What, then, can we say about Eucharist? The Eucharist is that sacrament which sustains us on our lifelong journey of conversion. Eucharist is the sacrament that connects, recapitulates, and intensifies the promises we have made in every other sacramental encounter. The Eucharist is the culmination of Christian initiation and the primary sacrament of reconciliation; it is also a sacrament of healing: "...only say the word and I shall be healed." And, if marriage, and indeed *every* vocation, is a matter of loving and dying, then it is the Eucharist which engages us in the dying and rising of all who love deeply and give themselves away for the sake of others.

Eucharist connects every one of the sacraments and continually invites us to remain faithful to the promises elicited by every other "Amen." The effect of our sacramental promises is cumulative. We celebrate the Eucharist as promise-makers, and as those who know their need of God and the nourishment of holy food and drink to live a faithful life. In Eucharist we celebrate the interconnection of our promise-making and promise-keeping across the sacramental spectrum: coming to faith, being newborn and beloved of God, gradually being conformed to Christ, the loving and dying of vocational choice and fidelity, reestablishing friendship with God after the rupture of sin, being joined to the sufferings of Christ, and, in the end, being returned by those who love us to God's tender care.

I spoke of this in a lecture not so long ago. I was describing the moment at the preparation of the table and the gifts when we bring all that we are and all that our "Amens" have ever promised, our joys and our sorrows, our everyday dyings and risings, and place it all there on the altar with the bread and wine. Then we pray that the Spirit will transform us just as really as the bread and wine, will merge our lives with that of Christ, will join us to the paschal mystery celebrated in every liturgy, played out in every person gathered at that table. I was stopped by a man who raised his hand to ask: "Besides you, who knows this stuff?"

That is a very important question!

Part IV

THE RECEPTION OF
THE LITURGICAL REFORM IN
THE UNITED STATES

"Besides you, who knows this stuff?"

That's the question that leads us to Part IV, an assessment of the strengths and weaknesses of the liturgical reform in the United States and the unfinished liturgical renewal launched at the Second Vatican Council.

I do not know if there has been any formal study worldwide of the vitality of the sacramental life of communities across the globe, though post-travel anecdotes suggest that reception of the reforms around the world has been very uneven. The kind of liturgical preparation and active participation endorsed by the council is barely evident in some countries but highly successful in other places. What *is* evident is that the church in the United States threw itself wholeheartedly into the implementation of the liturgical reform.

A good many years ago I had occasion to talk

with Father Balthasar Fischer, a German priest and scholar, founder of the Liturgical Institute in Trier, Germany in 1949, and the chief architect of the *Rite of Christian Initiation of Adults*. He told me ruefully that he had to come to the United States to see the RCIA enacted. In Germany, he said, it had been relegated to a sacristy shelf. Not so in the United States. There was genuine enthusiasm and receptivity to the new liturgy, at least at first.

Between 1969 and 1974, a five-year span of time, every major rite was translated into English, beginning with the Roman Missal. There followed: the *Rite of Christian Initiation of Adults;* the *Rite of Infant Baptism;* the *Rite of Confirmation*; the marriage, ordination, and profession rites; the *Consecration of a Church and an Altar*; the *Rite of Reconciliation*; the *Pastoral Care of the Sick and the Dying*; and the *Order of Christian Funerals*. Within a few years we were also in possession of the four-volume *Liturgy of the Hours*, the *Book of Blessings*, and *The Roman Pontifical*, as well as a variety of minor ritual books.

By any standards, this was an astounding new library tumbling off the presses! Admittedly, much of the work of translation was done in haste. Always there was the understanding that there would be a second generation of liturgical books prepared with greater leisure after an evaluation of the pastoral effectiveness of the original rites, the identification of need for original texts, and the desire for rearrangement of material to better serve the context of different countries that shared a common language.

Between 1969 and 1974 every major rite was studied, revised, approved, and then translated into the vernacular. In the case of the United States and other English-speaking conferences, this work was accomplished by the International Commission on English in the Liturgy (ICEL).[1] This new library of rites presented an overwhelming challenge for pastors in a short span of time. There were workshops and conferences and publications and parish programs. Organizations sprang up to support newly named diocesan directors of liturgy and pastors of parishes, musicians and artists, and newly minted liturgical ministers of every variety. And the new rites just kept coming.

The eucharistic liturgy was the first rite to be introduced. The *Rite of Penance* was, in 1975, the last major rite to be published, and it is my contention that it was never implemented or catechized at all. A few years ago, I tried to buy a copy of the *Rite of Penance*. I found it had been out of print for nine years so I went to Amazon.com. There was a copy there, available from a priest who said it was in mint condition—"never been opened." By 1975 there was already a fair amount of "change fatigue." A joke going around these days would have been apt in the mid-seventies. Question: How many

Catholics does it take to change a light bulb? Answer: Change???

In assessing the success of the liturgical reform, a first factor to consider is the speed with which the sacramental practice of the church was altered to its core and the ritual dislocation experienced by even the most enthusiastic liturgical aficionados in the wake of the reform. Ritual of any kind is highly resistant to change. It bears the story of the community, giving it shape and meaning, and the repetition of familiar patterns offers familiarity and a sense of security. The speed of liturgical change overwhelmed many.

A second factor is closely related. Because of that speed, the focus of catechetical instruction leaned largely on the mechanics of the rites. "Full, conscious and active participation in the liturgy, the rite and duty of every Christian in virtue of baptism," was, in large measure, equated with warm greetings of peace, full-throated singing, ritual postures, and energetic responses. Remember, in the earliest days there was even a commentator who told us when to stand and when to sit and what came next. We were preoccupied with more or less superficial liturgical details.

Largely ignored in this time of liturgical upheaval was a close reading of each new rite, especially the *praenotanda*, its "pre-note" or introduction, where the renewed sacramental vision, the theological foundation, and the pastoral implications of the rite had been spelled out so carefully by the members of the *consilium* who had been responsible for its creation. Ignoring the *praenotanda* would be like trying to assemble and operate a complicated machine without reference to the instructions.

Almost no one except priests and scholars even had access to this rich source of reflection. We were offered new wine through the lens of an older, even pre–Vatican II, theology. Lost in the telling was the intimate connection between sacramental experience and sacramental rites. Lost as well was a magnificent opportunity to catechize the mystery of Christ, bound up intimately with human experience, transforming every element of our daily "sacramental" lives by his life, death, and rising, and in the process making us a sign to one another—in life as well as in liturgy.

Has the liturgical reform languished because of the pressure and speed of its implementation and thus the compressed opportunity for genuine liturgical catechesis? Is it too late now?

A few years ago an insightful little book by Mark Searle was published posthumously by Anne Koester and Barbara Searle, Mark's widow. The book's title is *Called to Participate: Theological, Ritual and Social Perspectives*. Searle revisits the meaning of "full, conscious and active participation," demanded by the very nature of the liturgy, and he distinguishes three levels of active participation, each of which is progressively deeper and more demanding: participation in the ritual is the first level, participation in Jesus' death and rising is the second level, and, finally, participation in the mystery of the Triune God is the third level. These are three successively deeper invitations into mystery, three heart movements from the visible to the invisible, from the human to the divine. We participate in ritual prayer in order to participate in the priestly work of Christ on behalf of the world, and we participate in the trinitarian life of God and thus in God's work in human history. Full, conscious, and active participation has a scope and a breadth and a depth that is breathtakingly beautiful. It also makes enormous demands on us! But, as my friend in the audience asked, "Who knows this stuff?"

There is a recent study that helps us to gauge sacramental belief and practice today among Catholics.[2] The Center for Applied Research in the Apostolate (CARA) is a Georgetown-based organization that specializes in sociological research about the Roman Catholic Church. At the request of the United States Conference of Catholic Bishops, CARA produced a survey that studied U.S. Catholic participation in the sacramental life of the church as well as Catholic beliefs about the sacraments. The survey was conducted with self-identified Catholics. Major topics treated in the survey included: how Catholics have entered the church; the general sacramental lives of Catholics; the Mass and the Eucharist; reconciliation; anointing of the sick; ordination and vocation; religious devotions and practices in daily life; and general Catholic beliefs and attitudes.[3]

Here are a few of the survey's more significant findings:

- Of the seven sacraments more than 80 percent of Catholics find marriage, baptism, Eucharist, and confirmation somewhat or very meaningful.
- Catholics are *least* likely to say the sacrament of reconciliation is somewhat or very meaningful; 26 percent of Catholics say they participate in reconciliation once a year or more, while 45 percent say they never do so.
- Fifty-one percent of Catholics have requested the anointing of the sick for themselves or a family member, and women are more likely than men to say it is very important that they receive this sacrament.
- Older Catholics are more likely than younger Catholics to have celebrated their first reconciliation, first communion, or the sacrament of confirmation. With each generation the percentage having celebrated each of these sacraments decreases.
- Only 23 percent of adult Catholics say they attend the Eucharist weekly. Mass attendance is highest among Catholics who are older, female, married to another Catholic, have a college degree or more education, and attended Catholic educational institutions—especially a Catholic college or university.

- Only 12 percent of adult Catholics say they always attend Mass on a holy day of obligation and more than double that number, 26 percent, say they never do so.
- Of those who attend Mass weekly, the following are important: feeling the presence of God; prayer and reflection; and receiving the Eucharist.
- Of those who do not attend Mass weekly but do attend at least once a month, reasons for missing Mass include a busy schedule, lack of time, family responsibilities, health problems, or a disability. Those who attend Mass only a few times a year account for their choice by saying they do not believe missing Mass is a sin (64 percent) and that they are not very religious (50 percent).
- A majority of adult Catholics (57 percent) agree with the statement: "Jesus Christ is really present in the bread and wine of the Eucharist," and that number jumps to 91 percent of weekly Mass attendees. This leaves 43 percent of adult Catholics who do not believe in the real presence of Christ in the Eucharist.
- Eighty-three percent of Catholics say it is "somewhat" or "very" important to them that Mass is celebrated in language they most prefer, and 70 percent say it is similarly important that the Mass is celebrated in a way that reflects their ethnic and ancestral culture.
- Only six in ten respondents agree either "somewhat" or strongly" with the statement "Sacraments are essential to my faith."[4]

I have just offered a small sample of what this 178-page survey uncovered, all of it worth pondering for those who care about a flourishing sacramental practice built on the basis of sound theology and spirituality.

For me, the most startling of all CARA's findings is the last I listed above: that only six in ten self-identified Catholics believe that sacraments are essential to their faith. What can that possibly mean?

How is it possible that in all the efforts to introduce the reformed sacramental practices of the church we missed building a crucial theological foundation, namely, that the seven sacraments are simply seven ways of enacting with one another our participation in the life, death, and rising of Jesus and the transformation and divinization of our lives in his? To minimize the importance of sacrament is to minimize our own lives. We are, each one of us, a sacrament. We *are* sacrament from the day of our birth, and the baby lifted from the waters has become an image of Christ, filled with divine life, one more revelation of God with us, one more miracle of graced relationship.

Karl Rahner describes this reality in one of his exquisite prayers, this one in the form of a dialogue with Christ. In his meditation Rahner captures the amazing grace that in baptism we become a continuation of Christ's incarnation and a revelation of grace across space and time, always and everywhere. Through us Christ breaks through the limitations of his own earthly existence.

> When we were baptized, a new chapter in Your life began; our baptismal certificate is a page from the history of Your life. So we must fashion ourselves after Your image, You Who are the firstborn of many brothers [and sisters]. We must even "put you on." Since you live within us, Your image must become more and more manifest in us. God's hidden grace in Your human soul made your earthly life a pure expression and revelation of itself in the world of earthly phenomena. So too must this same grace—Your grace—make our lives, all that we do and suffer, a revelation of grace, and thus make our earthly life conformed to Your earthly and heavenly life. You wanted to live Your life in every age, in every situation, among all peoples and generations. Since You could not do this within the narrow confines of Your own earthly life, You take hold of our lives by Your grace and Your Holy Spirit. [The Spirit] comes to us through Your pierced heart to try to make our lives like Yours. In this way, O Jesus, Your life lives on in ever new forms and expressions always and everywhere until the end of time.[5]

From our baptismal day forward, sacramental living evolves in all the experiences that make up our "ordinary time" as we mature into adulthood: sickness, suffering, love and friendship, success and failure, joys and misunderstandings, ruptures in relationship, sin and reconciliation, caring for each other in the day-to-day, and accompanying one another at the point of death. The experiences of our ordinary lives are the stuff of sacrament, all of them transformed by what has happened in the life, death, and resurrection of Jesus.

Though we tend to use the language of sacrament for what happens in church, it is *all* of human experience that deserves the name "sacrament." As Thomas Groome has put it so well, the great sacraments are simply climactic celebrations of the sacramentality of life:

> God is present to humankind and we respond to God's grace through the ordinary and everyday of life in the world. In other words, God's Spirit and humankind work together through nature and creation, through culture and society, through our minds and bodies, hearts and souls, through our labors and efforts, creativity and generativity, in the depths of our own being and in the community of others, through the events and experiences that come our way, through what we are doing and what is "going on" around us, through everything and anything of life. Life *in the world is sacramental*—the medium of God's outreach and human response.[6]

Alas, in the forty-plus years since the council fathers conceived a renewed sacramental life, and despite the vision of an engaging sacramental spirituality found in the introduction to the individual rites, we have not yet clearly forged the bonds between rites and life. We haven't learned to make the connections. We have rolled out the reformed sacramental rites. In fact, we can do them very well. But we did not sufficiently ground them in the larger sacramental reality of our daily lives. We may enact the rites very well, but we miss the meaning altogether. Ultimately, until we can make the connections between the stuff of our daily life and the sacramental life of the community of believers, the implementation of the liturgical reform will remain sadly truncated and, in CARA surveys of the future, we may see a continued growth in the numbers of those who do not believe that sacraments are essential to their faith.

How do we learn to make the connections? How do we learn to see with "sacramental glasses"? How do we learn to pay attention? How do we communicate that sacraments are our life force and that becoming the sign to one another is our lifelong vocation?

Of course sacraments are essential! But, having been plunged into those baptismal waters, we tend to swim in them like fish who do not know they need the water to support and sustain their life. Only when we take baptism and membership in the community seriously and centrally can we come to recognize that those waters in which we are swimming are nothing less than our life force.

I remember reading a fragment in *Franny and Zooey* some time ago, a passage that I found so provocative:

> I'll tell you one thing, Franny. One thing I know. And don't get upset. But if it's the religious life you want, you ought to know right now that you're missing out on every single goddam religious action that's going on around this house. You don't even have sense enough to *drink* when somebody brings you a cup of consecrated chicken soup—which is the only kind of chicken soup Bessie ever brings to anybody around this madhouse. So just tell me, just tell me, buddy. Even if you went out and searched the whole world for a master—some guru, some holy man—to tell you how to say your Jesus prayer properly, what good would it do you? How in hell are you going to recognize a legitimate holy man when you see one if you don't even know a cup of consecrated chicken soup when it's right in front of your nose? Can you tell me that?[7]

Furthermore, making the connections is not just a new way of viewing reality. It also places demands on us to be ministers of that reality to one another in a variety of "priestly" activities. This is the "vocation" about which Archbishop Oscar Romero tried to teach his flock:

How beautiful will be the day when all the baptized understand that their work, their job, is a priestly work, that just as I celebrate Mass at this altar, so each carpenter celebrates Mass at his workbench, and each metalworker, each professional, each doctor with the scalpel, the market woman at her stand, is performing a priestly office! How many cabdrivers, I know, listen to this message there in their cab: you are a priest at the wheel, my friend, if you work with honesty, consecrating that taxi of yours to God, bearing a message of peace and love to the passengers who ride in your cab.[8]

You are a priest, my friend. Your daily work—your actions, your presence to others, the quality of your relationships—has the potential to touch, to nourish, to heal, to reconcile, to strengthen, to transform if it is done with integrity and love…the sacramental nature of all of reality makes your daily work revelatory of the divine. Sacramental living is all about making those connections.

It is in this context that I would like to consider the Roman Missal and the new guidelines for the translation of liturgical texts. We have recently been through a pretty divisive sea change regarding our liturgical translations. For thirty-two years the work of liturgical translation in the Roman Church was guided by a set of principles articulated in an instruction entitled *Comme le prévoit*, a document prepared by the Consilium for the

Implementation of the Constitution on the Sacred Liturgy in French and published in six languages to guide the translation of liturgical texts into the major world languages.[9]

In 2001 *Comme le prévoit* was superseded by *Liturgiam Authenticam: On the Use of Vernacular Languages in the Publication of the Books of the Roman Liturgy*. *Liturgiam authenticam* is a document prepared by the Congregation for Divine Worship and the Discipline of the Sacraments by mandate of the Supreme Pontiff, who approved and confirmed it by his own authority. The publication of these guidelines effectively stopped the confirmation of the missal of 1998, a second-generation translation of the Sacramentary by ICEL whose committees had devoted nearly ten years to its preparation. The principles articulated in *Liturgiam Auuthenticam* paved the way for the Roman Missal currently in use.

The contrast between these two sets of translation guidelines could not be more stark. According to *Comme le prévoit,* "...it is not sufficient that a liturgical translation merely reproduce the expressions and ideas of the original text. Rather it must faithfully communicate to a given people, and in their own language, that which the Church by means of this given text originally intended to communicate to another people in another time. A faithful translation, therefore, cannot be judged on the basis of individual words: the total context of this specific act of communication must be kept in mind, as well as the literary form proper to the respective language."[10] In making this judgment, *Comme le prévoit* adopted the principle of dynamic equivalence in contrast to a literal, word-for-word correspondence between the original and the translation. "A faithful translation," it said, "cannot be judged on the basis of individual words: the total context of this specific act of communication must be kept in mind, as well as the literary form proper to the respective language."[11]

Furthermore, the "unit of meaning," according to *Comme le prévoit*

> …is not the individual word but the whole passage. The translator must therefore be careful that the translation is not so analytical that it exaggerates the importance of particular phrases while it obscures or weakens the meaning of the whole. Thus, in Latin, the piling up of *ratam, rationabilem, acceptabilem* may increase the sense of invocation. In other tongues, a succession of adjectives may actually weaken the force of the prayer. The same is true of *beatissima Virgo* or *beata et gloriosa* or the routine addition of *sanctus* or *beatus* to the saint's name, or the too casual use of superlatives. Understatement in English is sometimes the more effective means of emphasis.[12]

By contrast, *Liturgiam Authenticam* adopted the opposite approach: "The original text, insofar as possible, must be translated integrally and in the most exact manner without omissions or additions in terms of their content, and without paraphrases or glosses. Any adaptation to the characteristics of the nature of the various languages is to be sober and discreet."[13]

At issue is whether a literal translation of a Latin prayer, however faithful to the text, can function in another culture, another country, another age, which has its own particular grammar and syntax customarily employed in spoken communication. Take, for example, the collect-style prayer. In Latin, this prayer is generally a single sentence including a relative clause, the *Deus, qui...*clause. In English, proclamation seems to demand that the prayer be rearranged and sometimes divided into two shorter sentences precisely so that the meaning of the text will be available to the assembly. Compare, for example, two different translations of the Latin collect for the Fifteenth Sunday in Ordinary Time.

Here is the translation from the new Roman Missal:

> O God, who show the light of your truth
> to those who go astray,
> so that they may return to the right path,
> give all who for the faith they profess
> are accounted Christians

the grace to reject whatever is contrary to the
    name of Christ
and to strive after all that does it honor.
Through our Lord Jesus Christ, your Son,
who lives and reigns with you in the unity of the
    Holy Spirit,
one God, for ever and ever.

By contrast, the 1998 *Sacramentary* provided this
translation:

O God,
you show the light of your truth to those who
    stray,
that they may return to the right path.
Grant that all who profess the Christian faith
may reject whatever is contrary to the gospel
and follow the way that leads to you.
We make our prayer through our Lord Jesus Christ,
    your Son,
who lives and reigns with you in the unity of the
    Holy Spirit,
God for ever and ever.

There used to be an important though unwritten
procedure in the ICEL process of translation and
evaluation. Before a draft translation was discussed in committee, it was prayed out loud. One
has to wonder whether that continues to be the
procedure of the present ICEL committee. We are
exposed almost daily to texts such as the first text

cited above whose internal coherence and meaning get lost in the length and complexity of a Latinate construction.

Much could be said about the new missal, but the context in which we are discussing it in this monograph is the conviction that there is an intimate connection between liturgy and life, between our daily life and our sacramental celebrations. In this context, my problem is not just with vocabulary like "consubstantial" or "prevenient" or "abasement," though such words seem somehow contrived and oddly out of place in the poetry of prayer. My concern is not simply a matter of archaism, or impossible syntax, or "...with your spirit." My sorrow is not simply the contradiction of a church eager to reach out to youth but now employing a language that youth find odd and slightly distasteful. My issue transcends the position taken by *Liturgiam Authenticam* that using inclusive language is a passing fad, foisted on the community by feminists though the church is the only contemporary institution that has not adopted inclusive language as its requirement in all forms of communication. My disquiet is not just that a unilateral approach to liturgical translation has voided thirty-plus years of ecumenical liturgical collaboration that produced a common translation of prayers such as the Gloria and the preface dialogue—prayers that, until Advent 2011, all major English-speaking

Christian bodies adopted and prayed using the same translation.[14]

Difficult as all of these results have proved to be, my concern is larger. I believe that because of this new translation we are being subtly distanced from the realities we have come to celebrate. My greatest struggle with the new translation is with the implicit suggestion that dignified, formal English is not quite good enough as liturgical speech; that God somehow prefers honorifics and Latinate constructions; that if we use the word "holy" as an adjective often enough—holy chalice, holy church, holy people—we will convince ourselves and God of the sacrality of the moment. The effect of this kind of language that we now employ is surely not going to help us "make the connections" between life and liturgy. In fact, just the opposite is true. The use of the new Roman Missal is going to make "making the connections" that much more difficult as more and more distance is created between the ministers and the assembly, between the altar and the dining room table, between sacraments and consecrated chicken soup.

Part V

BECOMING THE SIGN

We've covered a lot of ground. The Second Vatican Council, responding to its historical context, and thanks to the developments in biblical, theological, and liturgical scholarship and to the fruitful collaboration of bishops and scholars, produced a renewed liturgical practice rooted firmly in the two sacraments of Christ and church and in the daily sacramental experience of the divine in all of human experience.

Unfortunately, the implementation of this renewed vision stopped well short of its goal. Because of the speed of the reform, the sheer volume of innovations, and "change fatigue," the implementation of the renewed liturgy was often superficial. Although the richness of the church's sacramental understanding was carefully developed in the *praenotanda* to each of the revised rites, few presiders had the time to study them thoroughly and almost no lay Catholics had access to these ritual books or the inclination to curl up with them even if they did! New rites but an older theology has prevailed. The biblical warning about new wine in old skins should have alerted us that disappointment was all but inevitable.

And meanwhile, the Pew Forum study "Faith in Flux" and the CARA study of sacramental beliefs and practices among Catholics in the United States raise numerous issues and concerns for the future flourishing of Catholic sacramental engagement. Here are a few questions worth pondering:

- Why are Catholics leaving the church of their childhood and finding nourishment in other Christian denominations or other faith traditions?
- Will the faith community continue to dwindle in numbers?
- Will each succeeding generation of Catholics participate less in the church's sacraments, as is the trend at the present time?
- Will the clergy shortage in the United States and, indeed, throughout the West, adversely affect the availability of sacraments?
- Will communities welcome priests from other countries and cultures, especially when there seems to be a serious gap in social and cultural perspectives?
- Will belief in the real presence of Christ in the Eucharist continue to erode?
- If the sacrament of penance has a future, what form will it take and how will it reverse the loss

of meaning now experienced by nearly half of adult Catholics?

- Why have 40 percent of Catholics declared that sacraments are not essential to their faith and will this cohort continue to grow?
- Are Sundays and holy days "of obligation" obsolete, or is there a way to conceive of obligation as a personal commitment to sustaining the faith and life of the community of believers?

And, while not directly tied to these two recent studies but more to the thesis of these reflections, I would add these questions:

- How can we discover the relationship between experience and celebration so that they are mutually nourishing?
- Who will teach us that every "Amen" we whisper is a promise to become the sign in daily life that we have enacted in word and ritual action?

In light of these issues, I have three hopes and an impossible dream. My hopes include: an institutional commitment to sociological research in order to understand the deeper meaning and long-term implications of the sacramental trends unearthed in recent studies; a renewed effort at liturgical formation; and both personal and corporate commitment to "becoming the sign" by learning to make the connections between liturgy and life.

The impossible dream, with which I shall conclude, involves a fresh start altogether as a church of sinners in need of healing and hope.

Research

People who care deeply about the church's sacramental life need to probe more deeply the implications of the Pew Forum and CARA studies and others like them. On the face of it, both of these studies yield an enormous amount of data. Both are from highly reliable sources. The CARA study is particularly thorough in asking self-identified Catholics about their sacramental beliefs and practices and, with less success, some of the reasons why the respondents answered as they did.

The drawback to the CARA study is that it is a quantitative study. It has yielded numerical data that can be converted into numbers and percentages. So, for example, to use the statistic that most surprised me, 40 percent of respondents to the CARA study do not believe that sacraments are essential to their faith. The deeper question is why. Quantitative research cannot answer that question. The CARA study offers a snapshot of the Catholic community in the United States—numbers, percentages, comparative data. It does not provide insight into the reasons behind the responses.

The CARA study of Catholic sacramental belief and practice was commissioned by the USCCB. It is now nearly five years old. What happens to reports like this? Are there follow-up qualitative studies in the offing? Are focus group conversations planned? Are there supplemental surveys to ask the critical questions of those who responded to the previous survey? It appears, for example, that the sacrament of penance is in serious decline. We can read the statistics: 45 percent of adult Catholics report that they *never* participate in this sacrament. Again, why? What does it mean? No pastoral strategy is possible until we can understand better why people have formed their convictions or made their choices as they have. It is easy to read the results of a survey and develop our own conjectures, but with only anecdotal evidence from our particular circle of friends and acquaintances, such conjectures are useless.

When nearly half the respondents of the CARA study say they never participate in the sacrament of penance, a whole range of possibilities suggest themselves. Perhaps, for example, many Catholics have discovered that the Eucharist is the *primary* sacrament of reconciliation and consider penance something that is rarely needed. Or perhaps it is the case that this culture and age has lost a sense of sin and that such a cultural shift has made the sacrament unnecessary. I sometimes suspect that a good number of Catholics stay away from the sacrament because they aren't sure any more of how to begin and what to say and how to address what is aching

74

in their hearts and keeping them from being in good relationship with God. These are very different conclusions and would elicit very different pastoral responses. We simply don't have the data to make anything but educated guesses. Without good qualitative methods of research we are left to speculate about what the statistics mean and what pastoral response might be appropriate.

And what about the 43 percent of adult Catholics who do not believe that Jesus Christ is really present in the Eucharist? What do they believe? Is the problem one of language or of faith? Theologians speak about transubstantiation, a dollar word for our belief that while the accidents of bread and wine remain, the substance has been transformed into Christ's real presence. That's not easy for anyone to wrap her head around. Could we lead our communities through some mystagogical reflection on the presence of Christ that would make the reality of presence alive in the community—Christ alive in the word proclaimed, in the ministers, in the assembly, and especially in the bread and wine of the Eucharist, Christ's complete gift of himself that we might have life, and have it to the full?

I do not need to belabor this point. Serious study and dialogue about Catholic sacramental beliefs and practices would seem to be urgently needed, but who is doing it? Maybe this is a new opportunity for the close collaboration of bishops and scholars that was so tangible and so fruitful at the Second Vatican Council. Given the present climate of mistrust, that collaboration itself would be a sacramental sign.

Liturgical Formation

It seems obvious that the fiftieth anniversary of the Second Vatican Council provides a perfect impetus to revisit the council's teachings. We could use these next several years to address, in turn, some of the key documents of the council. People learn in different ways and with different motivations. Why not begin with storytelling so that post–Vatican II Catholics might be given a glimpse of what it meant to experience the council by those who lived through it? What if communities across the country invited the elders among them to talk about their experience of Vatican II, about what the church was like on the eve of the council, about the invitation of Pope John XXIII to throw open the windows, the expectations that built, the news coming out of Rome during those heady days, the documents developed by bishops from across the world with the help of their experts, addressing so many contemporary issues of urgent concern in the mid-twentieth century?

Against that backdrop, what if we talked honestly about the successes and the failures, the delights and the excesses of the sixties and seventies in the process of adopting new patterns of worship? What if we decided to start again to form ourselves in the liturgy and, at the same time, allowed the liturgy to form us in ever new ways?

I believe we need a new effort, not of liturgical *catechesis* but of liturgical *mystagogy*—a word used to describe the opening up of the mysteries for believers through reflection on actual experience. The early church made an important distinction between these two forms of teaching. When someone approached the community and asked to be welcomed into its midst, there was a prolonged period of catechesis, a time of no fixed duration when the candidate became familiar with the Christian way of life, with its teaching, its patterns of prayer, and its apostolic commitment. Candidates lived among Christians and prepared for their own profession of faith and the witness of their lives which they would promise as they joined the community.

Mystagogy, on the other hand, was less about teaching beliefs and practices. It generally took place *after* the experience of the sacraments of initiation and was more about helping the newly initiated go deeper into the mysteries that had been celebrated at the Easter Vigil. Mystagogy might include exploring such elements as the meaning of the darkness, the readings through the night, the experience of nakedness, the immersion into the waters of the baptismal pool, the trinitarian formula of blessing, the scent of the oil and the experience of anointing, the putting on of a new garment, the welcomed entry into a community waiting in prayer for their new members to appear, and the joy of participating fully at the eucharistic banquet.

We can learn much from this distinction between catechesis and mystagogy. In the words of the RCIA, *mystagogy* is understood today as the opportunity for neophytes to probe the mysteries of sacramental life:

> The neophytes are, as the term "mystagogy" suggests, introduced into a fuller and more effective understanding of mysteries through the Gospel message they have learned and above all through their experience of the sacraments they have received. For they have truly been renewed in mind, tasted more deeply the sweetness of God's word, received the fellowship of the Holy Spirit, and grown to know the goodness of the Lord. Out of this experience, which belongs to Christians and increases as it is lived, they derived a new perception of the faith, of the Church, and of the world....The distinctive spirit and power of the period of post-baptismal catechesis or mystagogy derive from the new, personal experience of the sacraments and of the community.[1]

What if we declared that *all of us are still neophytes*, baptized, yes, but still in need of liturgical formation, and specifically of that post-baptismal opening up of the mysteries we celebrate? What if we discerned the need for a specific period of mystagogy in our communities? What if we found ways of revisiting our sacramental experience, engaging in a holy remembering of the event, the words, the gestures, the objects, the sights and scents, the music and the silence? What if mystagogy became our bridge between experience and celebration?

This would be a new kind of liturgical formation, made up more of poetry than of prose, and it could be for the remaking of our sacramental experience if we let it work its way into our minds and hearts. What would it look like? A series of meditations, homiletic reflections, holy conversations, and poetry are among the several patterns of mystagogy available to us today.

1. Meditations

The meditations of Romano Guardini might suggest one possibility of liturgical formation useful for today. Guardini was an intellectual giant of the liturgical movement who discovered, as a young man, the centrality of the liturgy in his own life, and who fostered it in the communities he served.

Guardini believed that liturgical formation could not be successful if it simply used a historical approach, however interesting. People did not enter into the mysteries by learning how rites came into being and under what influences. Further, he noted that liturgy was not a series of ideas requiring learned interpretation. One did not learn to love the liturgy, he believed, by being told about it. No, one learned to love the liturgy by doing it well and, in the process, learning to pay attention to the simplest of signs.

One of Guardini's books, *Sacred Signs*, contains a series of mystagogical reflections on words and gestures and objects of the liturgy that have become familiar to us, and he makes them come alive again. Here is an example, a simple reflection on making the sign of the cross.

> When we cross ourselves, let it be with a real sign of the cross. Instead of a small cramped gesture that gives no notion of its meaning, let us make a large unhurried sign, from forehead to breast, from shoulder to shoulder, consciously feeling how it includes the whole of us, our thoughts, our attitudes, our body and soul, every part of us at once, how it consecrates and sanctifies us.
>
> It does so because it is the sign of the universe and the sign of our redemption. On the cross Christ redeemed humankind. By the cross he sanctifies us to the last shred and fiber of our being. We make the sign of the cross before we pray to collect and compose ourselves and to fix our minds and hearts and wills upon God. We make it when we finish praying in order that we may hold fast the gift we have received from God. In temptations we sign ourselves to be strengthened; in dangers, to be protected. The cross is

signed upon us in blessings in order that the fullness of God's life may flow into the soul and fructify and sanctify us wholly.

Think of these things when you make the sign of the cross. It is the holiest of all signs. Make a large cross, taking time, thinking what you do. Let it take in your whole being—body, soul, mind, will, thoughts, feelings, your doing and not-doing—and by signing it with the cross strengthen and consecrate the whole in the strength of Christ, in the name of the triune God.[2]

Guardini's *Sacred Signs* includes reflections on everything from doors and steps and linen to kneeling, standing, bread and wine, candles, incense, time and space sanctified, and even the name of God. The book was originally published in 1921, but prior to its publication Guardini had used these mystagogical reflections as the community gathered, before the Eucharist began. They were modest, focused meditations that he offered his assembly to deepen their knowledge and love of the liturgy and as a proximate way to prepare together for the Eucharist that was to follow.

Guardini also urged others, parents and teachers chief among them, to do their own reflections and to lead those in their care to the inner meaning of the rites. As he stated in his introduction, "…whatever in human nature responds to these elementary signs should be fanned into life."[3] Guardini was intent on helping people make the connections. Indeed, he "fanned them" into flame.[4]

The Center for Pastoral Liturgy at the University of Notre Dame, perhaps inspired by Guardini's work, published a more contemporary collection of such poetic meditations on the various symbolic words and gestures and objects of the liturgy in 1995. In reading them one cannot help but discover the richness and the depth of meaning in the most routine of our liturgical practices. Here, for example, is a meditation of the threefold signing before the reading of the gospel:

May the Word of the Lord live
in our minds and on our lips
and in our hearts.

We say it with a cross. Not a large gesture,
but a smaller one, like the anointing we received
when baptized into Christ Jesus:
binding our lives to his life,
    our crosses to his cross,
    our words to his words.

Three small gestures: not dramatic, not expansive;
but like most of our lives—
the daily efforts, the little ways
by which we strive to be faithful to the
        proclamation
of the Word in our speaking and loving and
        serving.

We say it with a cross,
the sign of our commissioning.
A reminder that the Lord's cross,
borne in pain but forever now
the emblem of life and love triumphant,
is engraved upon us
and we bear it for the world.[5]

There are other such collections,[6] and there is always the possibility that we might take the time ourselves to discover and articulate the meaning of these symbolic languages of prayer and fan into flame what they reveal to us of the interconnection of liturgy and our daily human religious experience.

2. MYSTAGOGICAL PREACHING

A second practice of liturgical formation is the practice of mystagogical preaching. The *General Instruction of the Roman Missal* directs the homilist to preach on the readings or another text from the ordinary or the proper of the Mass of the day, taking into account the mystery being celebrated and the needs of the listeners.[7] This offers wide latitude to a homilist to reflect over a period of time on the various parts of the Mass, on the texts of the prayers, and on particular ritual actions.

I remember being present for a mystagogical homily on Palm Sunday a couple of years ago. The focus was not on the palms but on the *procession*, on joining Christ whose face was set to Jerusalem, that place of suffering and of triumph. Just as we had processed around the church, we were encouraged to walk with Christ throughout the week, to be his companions on the road, to become intimately present to the various events of the passion of Christ as we hovered close by and watched and prayed.

I know my "walking" that week was of a very different kind from my normal routine. I contemplated what was going on in the mind and heart of Christ on this last journey. I shared his dread; I took strength from his resolution; I mostly watched and waited in silence as we walked together. I know others who heard the same homily and had an equally significant realization of the deeper mysteries we were celebrating during Holy Week and the events of the triduum because of being invited into the journey with Christ begun in the Palm Sunday procession.

3. Holy Conversations

Yet a third way of entering into the mysteries of the liturgy is to have the occasional opportunity to gather shortly after a liturgical experience to talk with other participants about what happened and how it may have touched and transformed members of the community. Was there a word or a ritual moment that stood out for one or another person? If so, why? Sometimes, for example, one can see a visible change in the person who has just received the sacrament of the sick. There is, after the sacrament, a sense of serenity and an attitude of acceptance about what lies ahead; there is consolation in the presence of Christ and the support of the community. The person being anointed can be quite articulate about what the liturgy meant to him or her and what particular moment stood out as revelatory of the consoling Christ in the presence of serious illness or the debility of old age.

Neophytes spend the whole of the Easter season reflecting on their experience of the Easter Vigil with others who have shared in the initiation liturgy. Does this suggest a practice that might apply to other sacraments? New parents, for example, might fruitfully talk about all the amazing connections between the baptism of their baby and how it somehow transformed their daily bathing and anointing and dressing of their new infant; they might also talk together about what it means in the nitty-gritty of the day-to-day that they have pledged to nurture the faith of their child and to give witness themselves of a baptismal way of life. Similarly, those who have recently been married or ordained could quite usefully reflect with others on the liturgical celebration of the sacrament and how that liturgy deepened their understanding of their sacramental commitment in the ordinary time of their lives. I am suggesting that the emphasis on sacramental preparation might find its mystagogical partner in a kind of sacramental "debriefing" among those with shared sacramental experience.

A few years ago I had a research grant to study how communities across the country had received the sacramental rites of Vatican II and how the rites were being experienced.[8] I found a willingness, even an eagerness, among parishioners to talk about liturgy, especially to have this conversation with a group of other participants. The insights of one person often touched another person in the group who may have had a wholly different experience of the same moment in the celebration. A reflection often began, "When such and such happened, I felt..." and others would chime in with agreement or surprise and then say what had been touched in themselves.

It was also a matter of great interest to me when some things were never mentioned. For example, after one very well attended communal celebration of reconciliation, no one mentioned the words of absolution. Though we call absolution "the form of the sacrament," these words apparently had little impact on the community. What stood out for the participants were the sheer numbers of people who had come to declare they were sinful and in need of God's mercy. What they found profoundly moving was the examination of conscience, the preaching, the music, and—above all—a laying on of hands in silence, which this community had borrowed from the rite of individual penance and incorporated into the communal rite. They didn't simply hear a formula; they said they *felt* forgiven and healed and full of hope.

People want to know why we do what we do. Further, many are more than willing to tease out the inner meaning of their sacramental lives and to discover anew or perhaps for the first time how life and liturgy are a seamless cloth. They simply need the opportunity provided for such "holy remembering."

4. POETRY

Yet one more form of mystagogical reflection available to all of us is found in the writings of poets who help us to explore the nature and geography of our human experience. Poets offer us a language of layered meanings and help us to discover our own emerging understandings. Think, for example, of Mary Oliver's poem "The Vast Ocean Begins Just Outside Our Church: The Eucharist."[9] Oliver names our experience of Eucharist…something has happened…the gifts of bread and wine are something else now…and something has been stirred in us…some desire has been tapped…a desire as vast as the ocean and as intimate as the presence which we desire, and doubt, and know within our bones—all at the same time.

Happily, the possibilities for mystagogical reflection on works of poetry are virtually limitless because all poets, in one way or another, excavate the terrain of human/religious experience—the great mysteries of life and death, love and loss, solitude and community as well as the simplest concerns and choices of our everyday lives. One need not search out particularly "religious" poetry, since it is all of human experience, pondered in poems, that sacraments name and celebrate.

I think it is true to say that catechesis is to mystagogy as prose is to poetry. The genius of the mystagogues—those who led the faithful in reflection on the mysteries—in the early church was their recognition that you cannot talk about an experience until you have had it—hence a period of mystagogical reflection *after* the experience of initiation. The equally important realization they had was that once you have had the experience, it is sometimes hard to find the right words to capture it. A perfect example of this is falling in love. Until that has happened to you, you can't talk with credibility about the experience. On the other hand, those who have fallen in love are notoriously unable to commit their experience to words. Poetry seems particularly suited to aid the probing of the mysteries for which words otherwise fail us.

These, then, are four fresh ways of doing liturgical formation: short meditations on the symbols, words, gestures, and movements of the celebration and what they may evoke in us; mystagogical preaching over a span of time; conversations about the liturgy to identify what may have moved us interiorly and why; and the use of poetry to open up the treasure that is our sacramental life. What sets these methods apart from the kind of catechesis that helped to implement the new liturgy just after the council is that this formation is aimed at believing and practicing Catholics who are familiar with ritual patterns but long to know more deeply what is being celebrated and how it connects with their larger sacramental universe.

Imagine the amazing consequences if the United States Conference of Catholic Bishops were to commit at least half as much time, energy, and resources in launching this kind of liturgical revitalization project as was expended on the introduction of the Roman Missal!

Paying Attention

Finally, while we hope for a renewed effort at liturgical formation and while we anticipate serious research on the community's sacramental practices, we need to accept our own responsibility for the way we live and participate in the sacramental life of the church. We need to work at making the connections for ourselves, even in the midst of our busy and distracted lives, and that means taking the incarnation seriously. The completely ordinary people who surround us and engage us, the myriad happenings of every day, the familiar objects like bread and wine and water and oil—and chicken soup—are revelatory of the divine if we can learn a kind of mindfulness and a new way of seeing. All of it forms the experience we bring to the celebration of sacrament.

Sister Mary Madeleva Wolf certainly took the incarnation seriously. She had that gift of paying attention and making the connections between life and liturgy in a seamless whole, as is clear in her poem "Bread and Wine":

> Seekest an altar, Lord? Take my awaking,
>   Alight with tapers kindled in the east,
> Decked with the dawn's full bud, to blossom
>   breaking.
>   Thy priest, O Lord—and who shall be thy
>   priest?
>   The dawn itself that lifts to Thee my
>   sacrificial feast.
>
> What sacrifice, what feast? Could I but borrow
>   The fruit of years that never may be mine!
> But all my folded life, my every morrow,
>   Change on this morning altar into Thine;
>   And let my soul's glad life be bread, my
>   heart's red love be wine.[10]

Madeleva, as other religious poets, had an uncommon gift of seeing and of being able to discover traces of the divine in all of reality and all of human experience.[11]

90

But how do we nurture that gift in ourselves?

Above we spoke of liturgical mystagogy as a deliberate choice to ponder the mysteries of the liturgy, to delve more deeply, to explore the experience of worship in such a way that we move beyond the surface signs to that which they signify. Liturgical mystagogy is a process that takes time and attentiveness, two items in short supply in our noisy, overcommitted, wired lives. Furthermore, we can't make the connections between liturgy and life unless we attend *both* to the deeper mysteries of the liturgy *and* to the deeper mysteries of our hearts.

Let's call this practice a "mystagogy of daily life"—a delving into the mysteries of our inner world, a discovery of the traces of the divine in the events and encounters of our day, the people we too often take for granted, the wonders of nature we sometimes ignore, the work that engages us, the joys and anxieties that fill our hearts, the moments when we know we have sinned as well as the times of light and peace. Ultimately, in order to make the connections between liturgy and life, we need to give equal attention to both.

The Christian spiritual tradition has always stressed the importance of making a review of the day, also known as the examen of consciousness in the Ignatian tradition. The examen is a prayerful process we use to explore the day's events and acknowledge where we collaborated with God and where we fell short in this precious relationship. The examen includes time for thanksgiving, a prayer for light, a review of the day, a response of gratitude or contrition as appropriate, and a time to look forward to and anticipate the day ahead. It concludes with prayer.

The value of this habit of daily reflection is that it helps us to notice and then to name the connections between our faith and our daily routine. Over time, this kind of daily reflection gives us greater access to the mystery of our inner world and the mystery of our life with God. And, again over time, this kind of regular spiritual discipline helps us to move closer to a life of greater integrity and purpose, a pattern of awareness, and an experience of conversion and new life. Gradually, imperceptibly, we "put on Christ," and we become a revelation of grace. We become the sign.

A Wild Dream

I conclude with what can only be called a wild dream, and yet I suggest it because I know the impact realized by a similar dream.

In late 1982 Joseph Bernardin was named archbishop of Chicago, where he would serve until his death in 1996. One of his first decisions was to lead a "mission" the following Holy Week. He hoped to reach the whole archdiocese by having the mission televised. A small group of men and women were invited to assist him in the planning of the mission and I was happy to be part of that group.

At first the conversations were about logistics. Then they turned to themes. Since the mission would be televised during the first few days of Holy Week, reconciliation became an important organizing theme. Scripture passages were suggested and pastoral approaches were offered. Some years earlier I had had an unforgettable experience of reconciliation that I shared with the group. I was part of a small group of women religious who met annually for an eight-day directed retreat, always with the same Jesuit director, though the group met in different areas of the country, depending on where we could find a place to accommodate us. At some point in the 1980s this retreat group decided to celebrate communal reconciliation and made simple preparations for an evening service. After we gathered and had sung an opening hymn, the presider knelt down in our midst and asked that we say the words of absolution over him. He said that before he could lead us in the sacrament of penance, he needed to acknowledge his own sinfulness, ask forgiveness of God, and be absolved through the ministry of the church. It was a shocking moment the first time it happened. We didn't think of ourselves in this relationship of mutuality, nor did we think of ourselves as "ministers of reconciliation," as Paul names the community in his second letter to the Corinthians. But our Jesuit friend was right in this as in so much else. We are mutual ministers in the church, never more so than when we become the sign to one another.

The Chicago mission began on the evening of Palm Sunday. Cardinal Bernardin was being broadcast at the same time as a showing of the hugely popular movie, *The Thorn Birds*, which cut into his viewership significantly! But those who tuned in to the mission will always remember the opening moments with the cardinal. Before he could preach a mission of healing and reconciliation, he said, he wanted to ask forgiveness for his own sins and failings. Furthermore, he knew that many people had been alienated from the church, so he also asked forgiveness for the times the church and its ministers had been a cause of scandal, for the times individuals had been treated harshly, for the ways in which love, forgiveness, consolation, and understanding had not been offered, for the times when the church had not been the face of the loving and healing Christ, welcoming all into his embrace.

In those few minutes at the beginning of the mission, Cardinal Bernardin became the sign. He wasn't just talking about reconciliation; he himself embodied sacrament.

Every single one of us has the same vocation.

NOTES

INTRODUCTION

1. Sister Mary Madeleva Wolf, CSC, *The Four Last Things* (Notre Dame, IN: St. Mary's College, 1986), preface to the 1959 edition.

2. The Pew Forum on Religion and Public Life, "Faith in Flux: Religious Conversion Statistics and Changes in Religious Affiliation," April 27, 2009. Among the Pew Forum's findings: "Catholicism has suffered the greatest net loss in the process of religious change. Many people who leave the Catholic Church do so for religious reasons; two-thirds of former Catholics who have become unaffiliated say they left the Catholic faith because they stopped believing in its teachings, as do half of former Catholics who are now Protestant. Fewer than three-in-ten former Catholics, however, say the clergy sexual abuse scandal factored into their decision to leave Catholicism." The mass exodus of Catholics is, however, masked in the statistics because the growing Hispanic population has kept the total number of Catholics in the United States at a steady state.

3. Mark M. Gray and Paul M. Perl, "Sacraments Today: Belief and Practice among U.S. Catholics" (Georgetown University: Center for Applied Research in the Apostolate, April 2008).

4. Constitution on the Sacred Liturgy (*Sacrosanctum Concilium*), 1.

PART I: THE COUNCIL IN CONTEXT

1. That very fact, a "church come of age," may also account for some of the difficulty in the implementation of the liturgical reforms. At the turn of the twentieth century members of an immigrant church had looked to the parish for cohesion and support, but members of a "church come of age" no longer looked to the parish for identity and cultural cohesion. When Catholics became part of the mainstream of American life, the parish began to compete with many other institutions for the presence, time, and attention of its members, commitments that it had once taken for granted.

2. Stephen Schloesser, "Against Forgetting: Memory, History and Vatican II," in *Vatican II: Did Anything Happen?* ed. John O'Malley (New York: Continuum International Publishing Company, 2007), 93.

3. For the first time, there was real-time coverage of a church council by the world press. Over a thousand press passes were issued for the four sessions. Near-daily press conferences kept the council before the eyes of the world and also assured a certain daily accountability on the part of the council participants. Both were unprecedented.

4. It seems that John XXIII was at least partially responsible for the style of the council's discourse. He is reported to have asked: "Seven inches of condemnations and one of praise: is that the way to talk to the modern world?" after taking a ruler to a page of the proposed agenda prepared by the curia for the approval of the

council fathers in anticipation of the opening of the council. See Peter Hebblethwaite, *John XXIII: Pope of the Century* (London, Geoffrey Chapman, 1984), 213.

5. Virgil Funk, "The Liturgical Movement," in *The New Dictionary of Sacramental Worship*, ed. Peter Fink (Collegeville, MN: The Liturgical Press, 1990), 695–96.

6. Pius X, *Tra le sollecitudini*, 1903, 28. Emphasis added.

7. See the Dogmatic Constitution on the Church (*Lumen Gentium*), 7.

8. Keith Pecklers, "Vatican II and the Liturgical Renewal," a talk delivered to the Federation of Diocesan Liturgical Commissions (http://www.fdlc.org/Liturgy_Resources/LITURGICAL_MOVEMENT-Pecklers.htm), 2.

9. In light of present-day tensions over the new translation of the Roman Missal, it is interesting to note that the first truly fierce debate at Vatican II was over the question of whether Latin should be retained as the language of liturgical prayer.

10. Anscar Chupungco, "*Sacrosanctum Concilium*: Its Vision and Achievements," in *Ecclesia Orans* 12, no. 3 (1996): 498.

PART II:
PRINCIPLES OF THE LITURGICAL REFORM

1. The principles articulated in this section have been culled from the Constitution on the Sacred Liturgy and, in some instances, from the revised sacramental rites. The author is responsible for their identification and ordering.

2. *Constitution on the Sacred Liturgy*, 5. *Documents on the Liturgy 1963–1979: Conciliar, Papal, and Curial Texts* (Collegeville, MN: The Liturgical Press, 1982), 5.

3. Ibid., 61.

4. Ibid., 7, summary paraphrase.

5. *General Instruction on the Roman Missal* (GIRM), 93.

6. *Constitution on the Sacred Liturgy*, 48.

7. GIRM, 95.

8. *Constitution on the Sacred Liturgy*, 7.

9. Ibid., 27.

10. *Dogmatic Constitution on the Church*, 11.

11. *Constitution on the Sacred Liturgy*, 10.

12. Ibid., 12–13.

13. Ibid., 14, 30.

PART III: SACRAMENT REIMAGINED

1. *Baltimore Catechism* (1891), 136.

2. *Catechism of the Catholic Church*, 1131.

3. *Rite of Marriage*, Introduction, 1.

4. *Rite of Christian Initiation of Adults* (RCIA), 78.

5. From the examination of the candidate in the *Rite of Ordination of a Priest*.

6. *Rite of Pastoral Care of the Sick*, 32.

7. Father in heaven,
   through this holy anointing,
   grant N. comfort in her suffering.
   When she is afraid, give her courage,
   when afflicted, give her patience,
   when dejected, afford her hope,
   and when alone, assure her the support of your
   holy people. Ibid., 125a.

PART IV: THE RECEPTION OF THE LITURGICAL REFORM

1. From the beginning of the work of translation, "mixed commissions" were established to assure a common text for countries sharing a common language. Conferences of bishops who spoke a common language appointed members to an international commission to prepare a single translation to be used by all countries using that language. Once a text was prepared it was sent by the "mixed commission" to all the member conferences for their individual review and eventual adoption.

2. Mark M. Gray and Paul M Perl, "Sacraments Today: Belief and Practice among U.S. Catholics" (Georgetown University: Center for Applied Research in the Apostolate, April 2008).

3. Ibid., Executive summary, 1.

4. Ibid., passim and paraphrased.

5. Karl Rahner, *Watch and Pray with Me* (New York: The Crossroad Publishing Company, 1966), 27–28.

6. Thomas Groome, "What Makes Us Catholic: The Sacramental Principle," *C21 Resources* (Spring 2012): 4.

7. J. D. Salinger, *Franny and Zooey* (New York: Bantam Books, 1961), 194.

8. Oscar Romero, *The Violence of Love*, compiled and edited by James R. Brockman, SJ (Farmington, PA: The Bruderhof Foundation, 2003), 24.

9. Published in *Notitiae* 5 (1969): 3–12. See also, *Documents on the Liturgy 1963–1979* (Collegeville, MN: The Liturgical Press, 1982), 284–91.

10. *Comme le prévoit*, 6.

11. Ibid.

12. Ibid., 12c.

13. *Liturgiam Authenticam*, 20.

14. *Prayers We Have in Common.* Initiated by the Consultation on Common Texts, a project that sought to provide a contemporary and ecumenical English version of prayers in regular use by the churches, common translation was taken up by the International Consultation on English Texts (ICET), which published *Prayers We Have in Common* in several editions between 1970 and 1975. These texts were then revised by ICET's successor, the English Language Liturgical Consultation, and published in 1988. ICEL collaborated in this work.

PART V: BECOMING THE SIGN

1. RCIA 245, 247.

2. Romano Guardini, *Sacred Signs*, trans. Grace Branham (St. Louis, MO: Pio Decimo Press, 1956).

3. Ibid., introduction.

4. The Catechesis of the Good Shepherd program (CGS) is a perfect example of Guardini's conviction that very young children can receive religious formation through all the symbolic languages of the liturgy and that the nascent religious sensibilities of the very young can most easily be fanned into flame. CGS takes a child's religious experience seriously and uses biblical and liturgical components to nurture that experience of God.

5. Janet Schlichting, OP, "Threefold Signing," in *Liturgical Gestures, Words, Objects*, ed. Eleanor Bernstein, CSJ (Notre Dame, IN: Center for Pastoral Liturgy, 1995), 13.

6. See, for example, Joachim Watrin, OSB, *Mass Symbols* (Collegeville, MN: Liturgical Press, 1947); John

Bradner, *Symbols of Church Seasons and Days* (Wilton, CT: Morehouse-Barlow Company, 1977); Balthasar Fischer, *Signs, Words and Gestures*, trans. Matthew J. O'Connell (New York: Pueblo Publishing Company, 1981); "Gestures and Symbols," *National Bulletin on Liturgy* 17:94 (May-June 1984); David Philippart, *Saving Signs, Wondrous Words* (Chicago: Liturgy Training Publications, 1996). Many of these texts could also serve as the basis for mystagogical preaching.

7. GIRM, 65.

8. See Kathleen Hughes, *Saying Amen: A Mystagogy of Sacrament* (Chicago, IL: Liturgy Training Publications, 1999). This book distills the mystagogical wisdom of worshiping communities about their immediate experience of worship.

9. Mary Oliver, "The Vast Ocean Begins Just Outside Our Church: The Eucharist," in *Thirst* (Boston, *Beacon Press,* 2006), 24–25. *The poem is also available in the preview of the Google e-book at* http://books.google.com/books?id=xUkAPHWJF68C &dq=%22Mary+oliver%22+AND+%22vast+ocean% 22&source=gbs_navlinks_s.

10. Sister Mary Madeleva Wolf, "Bread and Wine," in *The Four Last Things* (Notre Dame, IN: St. Mary's College, 1986), 24–25.

11. I have done a fair amount of thinking about how one learns to see and how one becomes more attentive to sacrament in the ordinary. Or perhaps it is better to reflect on how one sees the ordinary as sacramental, as revelatory of the presence and power of God and of the original goodness of all created reality. See Hughes, *Saying Amen*, chapter 2, "Paying Attention."